"The research-based ideas presented in this book can empower faculty and instructional designers to develop new and varied opportunities for collaboration and interaction in online courses. The specific recommendations provide practical solutions for overcoming common barriers to student engagement in the online environment. The authors deliver examples of online course activities that will inspire seasoned online instructors to experiment with different approaches and will motivate new instructors who may be hesitant to begin teaching online."

Dr. Melissa Rizzuto, *Director of Professional Development and Training, Florida SouthWestern State College, USA*

"*Best Practices in Engaging Online Learners* is a must-read for faculty and instructional designers who wish to improve the design and delivery of their online courses. The authors provide essential guidance on how to build and evaluate instructor presence and experiential and peer learning in online courses. I highly recommend this book for all who are interested in creating more engaged and meaningful learning experiences for online students."

Dr. Frederick Loomis, *Associate Professor of Higher Education, Pennsylvania State University, USA*

Best Practices in Engaging Online Learners Through Active and Experiential Learning Strategies

Best Practices in Engaging Online Learners Through Active and Experiential Learning Strategies is a practical guide for all instructors and instructional designers working in online or blended learning environments who want to provide a supportive, engaging, and interactive learner experience. This book explores the integration of active and experiential learning approaches and activities including gamification, social media integration, and project- and scenario-based learning, as they relate to the development of authentic skill-building, communication, problem-solving, and critical-thinking skills in learners. Readers will find guidelines for the development of participatory peer-learning, cooperative education, and service learning opportunities in the online classroom. In addition, the authors provide effective learning strategies, resources, and tools that align learner engagement with course outcomes.

Stephanie Smith Budhai is the Director of Graduate Education and an Assistant Professor in the Division of Education and Human Services at Neumann University, USA.

Ke'Anna Brown Skipwith is an Instructional Designer at Northeastern University, USA and completing her Ed.D in Higher Education Administration.

Best Practices in Online Teaching and Learning

Series Editor Susan Ko

Best Practices for Teaching with Emerging Technologies by Michelle Pacansky-Brock

Best Practices in Online Program Development: Teaching and Learning in Higher Education by Elliot King and Neil Alperstein

Best Practices for Flipping the College Classroom edited by Julee B. Waldrop and Melody A. Bowdon

Best Practices in Engaging Online Learners Through Active and Experiential Learning Strategies by Stephanie Smith Budhai and Ke'Anna Brown Skipwith

Best Practices in Engaging Online Learners Through Active and Experiential Learning Strategies

Stephanie Smith Budhai
and Ke'Anna Brown Skipwith

Routledge
Taylor & Francis Group

NEW YORK AND LONDON

First published 2017
by Routledge
711 Third Avenue, New York, NY 10017

and by Routledge
2 Park Square, Milton Park, Abingdon, Oxon OX14 4RN

Routledge is an imprint of the Taylor & Francis Group, an informa business

Library of Congress Cataloging in Publication Data
Names: Budhai, Stephanie Smith, author. | Skipwith, Ke'Anna Brown, author.
Title: Best practices in engaging online learners through active and experiential learning strategies / Stephanie Smith Budhai and Ke'Anna Brown Skipwith.
Description: New York : Routledge, 2017. | Includes bibliographical references and index.
Identifiers: LCCN 2016025370| ISBN 9781138670679 (hardback) | ISBN 9781138670686 (pbk.) | ISBN 9781138670679 (ebook)
Subjects: LCSH: Web-based instruction. | Internet in education. | Active learning. | Experiential learning.
Classification: LCC LB1044.87 .B83 2017 | DDC 371.33/44678—dc23
LC record available at https://lccn.loc.gov/2016025370

ISBN: 978-1-138-67067-9 (hbk)
ISBN: 978-1-138-67068-6 (pbk)
ISBN: 978-1-138-67067-9 (ebk)

Typeset in Minion
by Book Now Ltd, London

This book is dedicated to my children, Kingston and Kennedy. May this book serve as a reminder that there is no limit to what you can achieve.

Stephanie Smith Budhai

In loving memory of my grandparents, William and Inez Brown. Thanks for being my first teachers in life and for also inspiring me to "live boldly and to never settle".

Ke'Anna Brown Skipwith

Contents

Acknowledgments   xi

1   Engagement Beyond the Discussion Board   1

2   Experiential Learning (Cooperative Education,
    Internships, Practicums, Service-Learning,
    and Study Abroad)   13

3   Project- and Scenario-Based Learning   35

4   Gamification and Social Media   47

5   Building Social Presence Through Participatory
    and Peer-Learning Opportunities   61

6   Assessment of Active and Experiential Learning   73

References   91
Index   95

Acknowledgments

From Stephanie Smith Budhai

This book would not have been possible without my family of educators, especially Aunt Jackie and Uncle Reggie, who have inspired me to continue to hone on my pedagogical practices. To my mother, Charlotte, for your constant encouragement and unwavering support. For listening to long titles of articles and books I am working on and always seeming interested. To my husband, Winston, who never complains while I am always writing and who listens to me read drafts all of the time. To my colleagues at Drexel, Fred and Kristine, who gave me my first experience with online education. And to my co-author, Ke'Anna, for working with me and bringing your expertise in instructional design to this book. I would also like to thank Alex, for agreeing to accept our book proposal and for Richard, for answering all of the questions and getting us through the editing process from across the globe.

From Ke'Anna Brown Skipwith

I believe that education is the only vehicle through which doors of opportunities are opened and lives are changed. My experiences working and researching in higher education have enriched the passion and desire I have to serve people creatively and effectively – offering instructors and students a unique and personalized learning experience. Writing this book, has been my commitment to lifelong learning coupled with collaborative problem-solving, geared to help promote teaching and learning across the globe.

My participation in this book would not have been possible without the continuous support and encouragement of my mother, Robin. To my husband, Christopher, who inspires me daily to never lose sight of my *master* vision. I fondly acknowledge my tribe for cultivating a community that has kept me grounded and held me accountable throughout this wonderful endeavor. I will be forever grateful for your love, guidance, and energy that you have invested in shaping me into the woman I am today.

Special thanks to my co-author, Stephanie, for your dedication in embarking this journey with me and sharing your expertise in teaching and learning. In addition, thank you to the editorial and production teams at Routledge and Book Now for your patience and support while we worked to make this book a reality.

Finally, I am very thankful to my e-learning and instructional design network, colleagues (past and present), reviewers, mentors, sponsors, and my doctoral student experience. It is because of you that I am able to share these teaching strategies and best practices with the world. I am grateful for your insightful feedback on the various chapters and sharing your diverse lens of online and hybrid learning environments. It is my hope that this book will be a memorable moment in higher education that takes the focus off of the learning modality or tool and geared more towards improving the learner experience.

1
Engagement Beyond the Discussion Board

Towards a Paradigm Shift

There are many instructors already actively engaging their learners in the online learning environment. These are our champions and pioneers in this area, and we applaud their forward thinking. There are *some* who *may* think online education is independent work, with little opportunities for active learning and collaboration, or application of their learning in an authentic way. This type of thinking is highly detrimental to the integrity and reputation of online teaching and learning. Research has proven that frequent high-quality interactions between learners and instructors add to their success and serve as a learner engagement technique (Brinthaupt et al., 2011). This encourages us to change the way we are thinking in regard to interactions and engaging learners online. This book aims to facilitate idea sharing of ways to structure online courses with active and experiential learning opportunities.

Learning in the 21st century has drastically changed how learners access and process information. According to Quaye and Harper (2015), education is moving from a one-size fits all learning model and "dependency on sameness is no longer appropriate" (p. 3) for any learning environment. Learners need to practice and learn through experience (Dewey, 1938). Nursing instructors teaching online have used virtual clinical simulations (Aebersold & Tschannen, 2013) to provide learners with practice with making patient care decisions. Gamification has been used when teaching content that is traditionally unengaging, or to raise learners' interest. Both of these are examples of active and experiential engagement practices in online courses. Adapting and developing these high impact, deeper learning, active and experiential strategies that truly engage learners and connect them to course content prepares learners for making meaningful contributions to society.

Active and Experiential Learning Opportunities in the Online Classroom

Active learning and experiential learning are common terms, but often defined differently. The Association of Experiential Education (2015) defines Experiential Education as:

> a philosophy that informs many methodologies in which educators purposefully engage with learners in direct experience and focused reflection in order to increase knowledge, develop skills, clarify values, and develop people's capacity to contribute to their communities. (para. 2)

Experiential learning activities require learners to go beyond the confines of the online classroom and connect their learning to the real world, often making contributions to their future professional field and society. In traditional face-to-face on-campus programs and courses, learners often participate in different types of experiential learning activities that help connect their course content with real-world practice in their field. There are several types of experiential learning models including problem-based learning, project-based learning, service learning, and place-based education (Wurdinger & Carlson, 2010), as well as field experiences, practicums, internships, study abroad and inquiry-based learning. David Kolb (1984) has expanded on the instructional approaches of John Dewey by developing an experiential learning model that is comprised of four key components: Concrete Experience, Observation and Reflection, Forming Abstract Concepts, and Active Experimentation. We will discuss these in more detail in the next chapter.

Geographical constraints (Waldner, Widener & McGory, 2012), and time during the day are not impacted by experiential learning in online courses as course instruction can be carried out more flexibly. All of these experiences include a reflective piece, which could occur through the use of several emerging learning technologies.

Active learning is defined as an instructional approach that engages learners in the learning process. Through active learning, learners participate in meaningful activities "that involves them doing things and thinking about the things they are doing" (Bonwell & Eison, 1991, p. 2). Active learning techniques can be integrated into an instructor's lecture material no matter the size of the student population. Incorporating active learning in the classroom is crucial because it includes idea exchange and reflection in a non-hostile environment and might aid learners in understanding and articulating diversity of learning styles and needs.

Figure 1.1 illustrates the differences between active and passive learning activities based on a modification of Edgar Dale's cone of learning diagram. More specifically, it highlights how a student's learning experience (what they remember) can be organized not only around the type of learning activity that is being implemented in the learning environment but also how it relates to the learning outcomes (what they will be able to do at the end of the learning activity). Active learning as shown in this diagram focuses on activities such as hands-on experiences, collaborative and interactive lessons that have a real-world context as well as "learning by doing" or participating in authentic experiences. This active learning approach is helpful for online instructors as it can lead to a high retention of students learning valuable concepts that are tied to a specific event, experience, or learning opportunity. However, please note that passive learning activities such as reading and viewing lecture presentations/demonstrations are not less important and should not be ignored; it is recommended that they be coupled with active learning activities that helps reinforce the skills needed to understand the content.

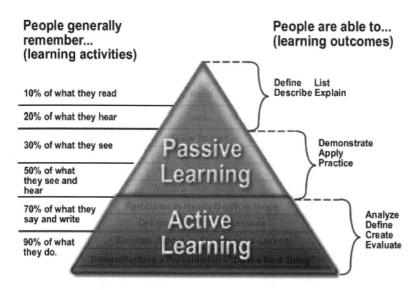

People generally remember... (learning activities)

10% of what they read

20% of what they hear

30% of what they see

50% of what they see and hear

70% of what they say and write

90% of what they do.

People are able to... (learning outcomes)

Define List
Describe Explain

Demonstrate
Apply
Practice

Analyze
Define
Create
Evaluate

Passive Learning

Active Learning

Figure 1.1 Dale's Cone of Learning

For example, several studies have shown that learners prefer using games, simulated virtual worlds, embedded videos with quizzes, role playing, and interactive case studies as active learning strategies to shape the evolution of a new learning landscape for online learners. Designing avatars or online characters in virtual worlds allows learners to experiment with alternate identities (Gee, 2004). These roles or "personas they assume in the game" (Jenkins et al., 2009, p. 47) represent different options for identities not only in the virtual world, but also in the real world. Thus, active learning and peer-to-peer interaction exposes its learners to multiple choices for self-identity which is necessarily a process in self-reflection and a valuable exercise in both social and work situations that generally leads to increased learning and understanding of a particular event or subject area.

Instructional design and active learning deal with motivation, challenge, individual learning styles, and social interaction. Learning outcomes and goals set by instructors are closely related to the goals presented in gamification, simulations and interactive learning platforms. These examples of active learning not only cultivate learner development, but also enhance skills needed in education such as team building skills, problem solving, critical thinking, analysis, and so on. In addition, active learning opportunities create authentic opportunities for 21st-century learners to build on previous knowledge and develop in-depth knowledge and skills. When instructors incorporate active learning strategies that are closely tied to desired learning outcomes, learners are able to transform practical experiences into the classroom environment. For example, game-based learning applications, and experiential learning opportunities coupled with online learning platforms have created many possibilities for sharing and transferring knowledge and information to learners especially in the online environment to meet the required learning performance goals and standards.

In this section we shared just a few ways instructors can teach using active and experiential learning strategies. Throughout the book, a plethora of different activities and teaching tools will be shared. Many instructors and instructional designers do not actually know where to start when thinking about how to create online classrooms that parallel the teaching and learning present in many classrooms. Some instructors are hesitant to teach online (Ward, Peters & Shelley, 2010) and there is still a belief that online courses cannot provide the same rigor as traditional campus courses.

Rationale for Engaging Online Learners

We have found that online education environments provide opportunities for exciting and innovative experiences. It is difficult to imagine that learners who learn online could be passive consumers of content. Michelle Pacansky-Brock (2013), argued that one of the difficulties that college instructors face is low engagement and motivation in the classroom. Instructors and instructional designers all experience similar difficulties with actively engaging learners in online courses. It is important to cultivate a learning experience online that learners enjoy, and want to be part of. Additionally, retention and attrition is always a topic of substance, and 32 percent of the post-secondary population are online learners (Allen & Seaman, 2013). It is also important to recognize that online learners are more at risk of feeling isolated psychologically from the course experience (Bigatel & Williams, 2015). Interestingly, despite all the innovation and creativity that has surfaced in the last decade surrounding online teaching, many still rely on traditional practices such as lecture and discussion.

The active and experiential learning strategies that we employ in traditional courses can be, and already are being, translated into the online course environment by many instructors and instructional designers. This book was written to share some of those examples and provide a comprehensive toolkit complete with pedagogical strategies for integrating active and experiential learning into online courses. You may be asking: why move a traditional course that is already well structured and actively engages learners into the online environment? There may be a course that a instructor has taught for years in the traditional classroom setting very well, but due to demands from administration to offer more courses online, or a personal interest of the instructor to instruct in a different setting, the course may be delivered online. While the availability of robust Learning Management Systems (LMS) has helped streamline the process of translating content and learning activities into the online environment, structuring the course to match the level of engagement and learner interest typically present in a traditional course and developing learning activities that allow learners to be full, active participants in their learning process, can present some challenges.

Aside from ensuring pedagogical soundness in online courses, competition from a wide variety of online programs can be a catalyst for rethinking about how we shape our online classrooms. Learners seek online learning experiences that go beyond reading words on a computer screen and responding to questions by typing their response. While it adds an interesting interactive component to the course, the discussion board does not necessarily create a course that is designed with active and experiential learning in mind, and is often an element overly relied upon. Learning activities that allow for going beyond the discussion board provide more intentional opportunities for learners to actively engage in their own learning. We see these active and experiential learning opportunities as what a marriage between the upper echelon of Bloom's Taxonomy of Higher Order Thinking (Bloom, 1956) and the major tenets of John Dewey's theory of experiential learning (Dewey, 1938) would look like. The way in which content is presented and how opportunities for learners to engage with content must be grounded with these two in mind. Learners must have the chance to learn while doing in the online classroom in order to create, produce and evaluate, and access deeper learning experiences (Czerkawski, 2014).

The opportunity to receive course content online has allowed for several populations of learners who would not have previously had the opportunity to access a post-secondary course. Although typed text and traditional lecture materials are overused in online courses, limiting the interactions learners can have with each other, the instructor, and course content (Hirumi, 2002), the available learning technologies can help facilitate online educators in interacting with the course content, each other, and the instructors in new and innovative ways. By rethinking pedagogy in the online classroom and incorporating a host of active and experiential learning strategies, these things can come to fruition. The question is not whether the quality of instruction and learning experiences can be maintained in the online classroom. The question is, how can instructors and instructional designers build courses that encourage deeper learning (Czerkawski, 2014) while fully engaging learners in the learning process? We answer this question in this book by providing a host of active and experiential learning strategies that can be integrated in the online classroom. In addition, simple, practical, and ubiquitous emerging technology tools that support the integration of active and experiential learning strategies that can be leveraged are explored.

Opportunities for Flexible Learning Environments

Today, online learning has allowed higher education institutions to reach a more diverse and global learner population. According to Allen and Seaman (2013), over 7.1 million of higher education students are taking at least one online course. This growth in online enrollments has increased by 3.7 percent since 2014. Online learning is also providing learners with flexible learning opportunities that suit their busy lifestyles, providing affordable financing options, as well as accessibility to connect with their instructors and classmates across the world. This flexibility means offering different formats and different modalities of taking courses. A synchronous online course structure does not immediately translate to a more engaging learning experience than asynchronous. There are limitless ways to actively engage learners in online courses in all types of formats.

What is the main difference between asynchronous and synchronous learning in an online environment? The asynchronous learning model is self-paced and allows the learner to complete the course materials at their own pace. Instructors working within this learning modality can post course lectures, assignments and knowledge checkpoints that are completed individually by each learner. However, learner interaction in *many* asynchronous environments solely takes place through the discussion boards and other designated areas using the LMS tools (e.g. blogs or wikis) assigned by the instructor where the learners are required to provide a response or feedback to one another (no collaboration is needed prior to their individual postings). Creating opportunities for active and experiential learning can help ameliorate the lack of collaboration and engaged activity in asynchronous online courses.

The synchronous learning model inherently requires active learner participation with the instructor and their peers that occurs at specific dates and times throughout the duration of the course. Learners are required to attend and participate fully in synchronous learning activities and assignments. Instructors working within this learning modality can also post course lectures and assignments as seen in the asynchronous learning environment. However, the key difference in synchronous learning is that it provides multiple ways where instructors and learners can share, collaborate and exchange knowledge in a virtual platform (e.g. real-time class discussions, live group collaboration, etc.) no matter the distance between them. Learning in the 21st century calls for online learning environments to be participatory that does not depend on the learning modality (e.g. asynchronous or synchronous).

Online educators must create instructional strategies that cater to not only the diverse learning styles, but also their learning comprehension and capacity. Some learners may prefer to go through the content multiple times, which can result in them taking longer to complete the content within a given timeframe. Other learners may prefer to get through the content more quickly. Today's learners are acquiring useful skills through participation in these types of learning environments. In addition, this can be beneficial in how an individual's online experiences can be used not only to facilitate learning, but also to assess learning outcomes and abilities in the classroom. When learners are engaged in these types of activities, learning takes place – mediated by the online access, resources and community contexts that will support learners by giving them the best learning options and experiences. Through active and experiential learning activities, these quality interactions present in synchronous online courses can be incorporated in asynchronous online courses by alternating the focus of the learning activities.

The Need for a New Type of Learning Space for Learner Engagement

The evolving landscape for learning in the 21st century includes participatory cultures. This inclusion may or may not be recognized by the entire community of online educators, but it exists with or without such acknowledgement. In this age, the computer is referred to as "a magic black box with the potential to create a learning revolution" (Jenkins et al., 2009, p. 6). With a learning revolution at our fingertips, it is important to take advantage of the current learning opportunities. Gee (2004) describes participatory cultures – termed as "affinity space" – or "communities of practice", where learners share their creations and take part in the membership of that community. For example, in online learning, this type of learner interaction and exchange of ideas does not occur in the traditional discussion board area. During this process, learners are learning while doing, and they receive essential feedback as they go along – affinity spaces are where learning occurs. Gee (2004) mentions that learners learn best when their learning is part of a highly motivated engagement with social practices that they value. Affinity spaces or participatory cultures are created and controlled by the learners and facilitated by the instructor. It is the learners that determine what type of content to interact with, which learning tools can reinforce learning goals of the subject matter, and so on. In this sense, participatory culture can be viewed as an affinity space for learning, for it is the space where content of the subject matter is transformed by the interactions of the learners in the learning environment. Instructors can include the participatory culture or affinity space approach into instruction by shifting the focus of learning from an individual assignment such as the discussion board to community interaction with the course materials. Simply put, this new approach allows new ways of communicating and synthesizing information and all learners should be exposed to these emerging active learning trends. As methods for learning expand, it is important to seize opportunities to teach and share methods for engaging in participatory culture to ensure that learners are aware of these new and emerging tools and strategies.

Moving Forward with Active and Experiential Learning Strategies

We hope that the content of this chapter has excited you about continuing or starting to reframe the online class environment to include active and experiential learning and move online learners from being passive consumers of information, to active participants of their learning. The following chapters will provide more details on how to incorporate active and experiential learning strategies into online classrooms, with examples covering various disciplines. Chapter 2 covers experiential learning in more depth with focus on practicums, co-ops, studying abroad and service-learning. Chapter 3 explores project and scenario-based learning as well as virtual labs. Chapter 4 discusses gamification and social media. Chapter 5 examines organizing and facilitating participatory and peer learning and building social presence, while managing the inherent challenges of them. Chapter 6 focuses on how to assess learner engagement and active learning to ensure that the strategies we are employing are effective and positively impacting the learning environment. Throughout each chapter are examples of active and experiential learning strategies in all disciplines and templates for getting started.

2
Experiential Learning (Cooperative Education, Internships, Practicums, Service-Learning, and Study Abroad)

Experiential Learning

Over the last century, experiential learning has been the subject of much research. Engaging with the community (Dewey, 1915), reflective thinking, and learning from experience (Dewey, 1933) are some of the major tenets of experiential learning as presented by John Dewey. In order to create authentic learning experiences for learners, opportunities for experience must be integrated with education to create a unique non-formal learning experience for learners to learn while doing (Dewey, 1938). This holds true too for courses that are delivered in online formats. Dewey (1938) held the "belief that all genuine education comes from experience" (p. 13) and that through the experiences that learners would receive as a result of "learning by doing", they would grow and develop to be active members of society.

Kolb (1984) added to the work of Dewey and presented a model for understanding the process of experiential learning through a four stage cycle: Concrete Experience, Reflective Observation, Abstract Conceptualization, and Active Experimentation (see Figure 2.1). In the concrete experience stage, learners experience and participate in a new experience or a familiar experience in a different way. In the next stage, reflective observation, learners have the opportunity to reflect on the experiences gained in the first stage to think and reflect on their experience. Abstract conceptualization is when meaning is made from what the learners thought about in the second stage. In the final stage, active experimentation, is the application piece. Learners take the experience they have through experiential learning and apply it in their real lives and future professions.

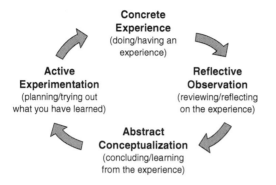

Figure 2.1 Kolb's (1984) Experiential Learning Model

According to the Association for Experiential Education (2015), Experiential Learning is defined as:

> a philosophy that informs many methodologies in which educators purposefully engage with learners in direct experience and focused reflection in order to increase knowledge, develop skills, clarify values, and develop people's capacity to contribute to their communities. Experiential educators include teachers, camp counselors, corporate team builders, therapists, challenge course practitioners, environmental educators, guides, instructors, coaches, mental health professionals ... and the list goes on. It is often utilized in many disciplines and settings: Non-formal education, Place-based education, Project-based education, Global education, Environmental education, Learner-centered education, Informal education, Active learning, Service learning, Cooperative learning and Expeditionary learning.
>
> (para. 2)

Types of Experiential Learning

Cooperative Education (Co-Op)

Similar to internships in that learners complete their experience in a professional work environment related to their career goals and profession, co-ops are usually longer than internships, 6–12 months, and learners are typically competitively compensated. The Cooperative Education and Internship Association (2015) define cooperative education as:

> a structured method of combining classroom-based education with practical work experience. A cooperative education experience, commonly known as a "co-op", provides academic credit for structured job experience. Co-op experiences are either full-time (40 hours per week) alternating periods (semester, quarter) of work and school or part-time (20 hours per week) combining work and school during the same time period. Co-op experiences are paid, supervised by a professional who has followed the same career path of the student and students complete more than one assignment (2 or more) with progressive levels of responsibility.

Some institutions have co-op experiences embedded as a requirement for learners in all academic programs, while other institutions may only require it for business and law students. Completing a co-op experience while completing other courses online is a very attractive option because learners can take more courses while working during the day at their co-op site.

Internships. An internship is a short-term experience, paid or unpaid, that provides learners with real-world experience in the profession they are hoping to be part of upon graduating with their degree. The National Association of Colleges and Employers (2011) define internships as:

> a form of experiential learning that integrates knowledge and theory learned in the classroom with practical application and skills development in a professional setting. Internships give learners the opportunity to gain valuable applied experience and make connections in professional

fields they are considering for career paths; and give employers the opportunity to guide and evaluate talent.

(para. 6)

To complete an internship, an accounting major may spend six weeks during the summer as an intern at an accounting firm, or a nursing major may spend a semester interning at a clinic. Internships have a defined start and end time, or number of hours, and learners are supervised by a site manager and their instructor. Learners typically receive college credit for their internship experience, but may not go to class regularly during the time they are completing their internships.

Practicums. A practicum is an experiential learning experience where learners go out in the field to experience the work of the major they have chosen. Practicums are short-term experiences and typically last a few hours a week or month, throughout the course. Practicums are generally not paid experiences, but they are connected to course content. Learners are usually required to complete field reports based on their experiences at the practicum site.

Service-Learning. Service-learning combines service to the community and reflection, with course content. Jacoby (1999) defines service-learning as a "form of experiential education in which learners engage in activities that address human and community needs together with structured opportunities intentionally designed to promote student learning and development" (p. 20). Service-learning is distinct from volunteerism or community service as it is directly connected to a course and typically learners receive academic credit for completing their service-learning experience as part of a course. There is also a critical reflection piece required for service-learning courses that serves as a mechanism for learners to think deeply about their civic commitment in relation to the course content. It is important to note that the purpose of service experiences for learners is to carry out similar jobs in the chosen professions for which they are presumably attending college. Learners are not paid for their service-learning contributions.

Study Abroad. Study abroad is an experiential learning experience where learners travel to a foreign country to study, learn and develop. Typically, study abroad experiences have a distinct focus, for example, to practise a language, learn about global affairs, or study the country's educational, business, law or health system. Study abroad experiences can range from one-week short-term experiences to one-year experiences. Depending on the length of the service experience, the number of credits that a learner will take and the intensity of the course that the service experience is being required of, will vary. Study abroad experiences can also include an internship component, particularly when a learner's major has an international affairs focus.

We created Figure 2.2 in a tool using wordle.net and it serves as a visual separation between subtopics. This could be used as a header for an online course to pull together visuals that display some of the major concepts of the course.

Figure 2.2 Importance of including experiential learning opportunities in online courses

Note: This image was created on http://www.wordle.net/

It is important that learners taking online courses have the ability to benefit from some of the experiential learning experiences they would normally participate in, in a traditional bricks and mortar course. The physical presence of the instructor and other learners is not always possible in online courses, and interactions between people can be more limiting in an online course (Abedi & Badragheh, 2011). By including experiential learning into online courses, we can prevent learners from feeling "eSolated" (Apanna, 2008, p. 15), and provide them with various engaging ways to connect with course content. This includes:

- **Making real-world connections** (Jacobson et al., 2011): In addition to communicating with other online learners who are located in geographically separate locations around the globe, experiential learning can provide opportunities for learners to engage in their local communities or area and make connections with others. By going into field-experience or practicums, learners see what is going on in the world and have the opportunity to think about how what they are studying in the online classroom interacts with it. Learners then bring that experience back into the online forum, share those experiences with their classmates, and make further meaning of it when presented with future content.
- **Hands-on experience** (Abedi & Badragheh, 2011): Part of learning involves hands-on practice. This is particularly true in fields such as Nursing, Education, Medicine and Accounting. Learners, regardless of the forum used to disseminate content, should have the opportunity to put their learning into practice. Internships and apprenticeships are great experiential learning opportunities for learners to practise nursing techniques, pedgogicial skills for education majors, and mathematical computations.
- **Practice at professionalism:** An extended practical experience such as a co-op would allow learners the opportunity to

be in a similar professional work environment to the career the degree they are earning leads them towards. There are some professional and ethical practices that must be learned on the job through others and within the work context. Co-ops, being more extended in nature than internships, can help learners grow and develop their professional and ethical skills, while gaining useful experience that can be added to their resume.

- **Social interactions:** There are many ways to build social presence (Garrison, Anderson, & Archer, 2001) in online courses, and because online learners do not have opportunities for a traditional campus experience, it is important to provide ways learners can interact with others outside of their online classroom. Any of the types of experiential learning activities (e.g. study abroad, clinical field experiences and internships) would allow learners to interact with others in meaningful ways, while learning. The site that the learners are on, becomes the "campus" in a sense.

- **Civic contribution:** Service-learning experiences embedded within an online course can provide learners with the opportunity to tackle worldly issues, while learning. Guthrie and McCracken (2010) have identified the combination of online instruction and service-learning as opportunities "to be individually and collectively relevant" (p. 79). John Dewey's work on active citizenry is relevant and present today. This is one of the areas of development for college learners and learning and experiencing how to be active members of society, and making meaningful contributions. Learners in online courses should have the same opportunity.

We have laid out above what experiential learning is, the many different types of experiential learning, general outcomes of experiential learning for learners, and the importance and impact areas experiential learning can have within an online class. What is provided next are several examples of experiential learning activities in different academic disciplines, and an integration of how different types of web 2.0 and multimedia applications within and outside of learning management systems can be leveraged to connect the experiential learning activities to the online course content.

Table 2.1 provides examples of the types of experiential learning activities in different academic disciplines.

Technology Tools to Leverage in Facilitating Experiential Learning in Online Courses

Vlogs, virtual blogs and journals

Vlogs, virtual blogs, and online journals are essential multimedia tools that learners in online courses completing an experiential learning activity or experience can use to document their experiences. Vlogs are video versions of blogs that include some sort of video and picture content. Vlogs use audio and video to capture the thoughts and facial expressions of the person creating the vlog. There is something powerful about seeing and hearing a learner's reactions, and a vlog can provide this type of experience. Blogs are a collection of personal thoughts written in an informal way that is publicly shared on a website. Instead of using audio and video, words are simply typed to get across the person's thoughts and ideas. Sometimes pictures are added to blogs as well to complement the words. Online journals are private spaces housed online with the words, thoughts and ideas of someone. Many learning management systems have an online journal feature embedded as an optional tool, but there are free multimedia apps that can serve the same purpose. Vlogs, virtual blogs, and online journals can be incorporated in a variety of ways with experiential learning activities. For example, they can be used in the following ways, for different types of experiential learning:

- **Reflecting on the service experience** (Service-Learning): One of the ways service-learning is different from community service is the required reflection piece that takes place within a service-learning experience. In a typical bricks and mortar

Table 2.1 Examples of the types of experiential learning activities in different academic disciplines

Academic discipline	Co-ops/Internships	Service-learning	Study abroad
Business	Co-ops and Internships for business majors may include working in the following types of offices/positions: • Accounting majors could complete a co-op/ internship at an accounting, tax, or other business firm where they are exposed to accounting practices • Administration majors can complete a co-op/ internship where they have the chance to work under someone on the leadership team at a business, and	Learners can partner with non-profit organizations in their communities or communities near them, where their service would be related to the business profession, specifically the course they are in, but have a direct or indirect impact on at-risk, low-income, and/or marginalized communities. Activities could include: • Accounting majors could work at a tax-agency to provide support to low income residents who cannot afford to pay a tax professional • Business Administration majors can prepare a business plan for an understaffed non-profit organization whose mission is in social justice • Foreign Policy majors can work with organizations that support refugees and those seeking political asylum	Business majors may spend their study abroad experience engaging in the following: • Researching the local government policy of the county they are in • Work with larger international organizations such as the United Nations

(Continued)

Table 2.1 (Continued)

Academic discipline	Co-ops/Internships	Service-learning	Study abroad
Education	Co-ops and Internships for education majors may include working in the following types of organizations: • Educational Policy majors can complete a co-op at a education-based organization • Special Education majors can complete an internship at an agency that does special education law and policy work • An early childhood education major can complete a co-op at a playgroup or recreation center where they create programming for young children	Education majors can serve within the different types of educational institutions whose work connects with the course they are completing the service-learning experience in: • Early Childhood Education majors could complete service in an early learning center working with marginalized young children and their families • Educational Policy majors can complete the service portion of their course in a non-profit organization whose missions surround educational policy. Activities could include researching policy, interpreting policy, and drafting policy reports for the organization • Higher Education majors can serve at community colleges or their local higher education board • Secondary Education majors can complete their service in local middle and high schools in low-income under-resourced districts • Special Education major can work with local early intervention agencies to support children with exceptionalities. Learners can serve as one-on-one support professionals or companions to learners with special needs who are hospitalized with various health impairments	Experiences for education majors who study aboard can include: • Working with English Language Learners and teaching English • Visiting different foreign countries to examine their educational systems

Health Professions	There are endless opportunities to create meaningful service-learning opportunities for learners whose major is within health professions: • Athletic Training • Public Health • Pharmacy • Physical/Occupational Therapy • Medicine • Nursing All of these majors would be able to work in low-income neighborhoods providing care based on the specific field that they are in	Co-ops and Internships for education majors may include working in the following types of organizations: • Working for a school to develop healthy activities and lessons for learners • At a home health education providing basic care to elderly people • Providing triage care to veterans at a VA hospital	Nursing, Physical Therapy, and other Health Professionals can complete a study abroad experience in both developing and first world countries to learn the different ways of providing medical care. Some of the best medical education programs are abroad and would prove to be beneficial for learners.
Human Services	Human Services fields are generally already geared towards working with at-risk, low income, and/or marginalized communities. • Criminal Justice • Counseling/Psychology • Social Work	Co-op experiences for Human Services majors can be in any non-profit organizations that focuses on issues of human rights	Social work majors can travel to foreign countries to build homes and get involved in social justice and humanity issues related to the rights of all people

Figure 2.3 An example of how VoiceThread can be used as a learning tool to emphasize a point with the doodling feature and to use video and voice while reflecting on a service experience within an online class

Source: Image used with permission of Voicethread

classroom, learners are given the opportunity to reflect in the classroom setting, sharing their experience with their classmates and teachers. Learners can record their reflections on a vlog or virtual blog and then post within the online course shell or using a multimedia tool such as Voicethread (see Figure 2.3). This can provide learners taking an online course with a service-learning component with the opportunity to complete their reflection and share their experiences with their classmates and instructor. If the instructor would like to have the learners reflect privately, where only the instructor can view, online journaling can be used. This is a feature that is usually embedded in learning management systems. The online journal feature is similar to a digital blog, with the exception that it will not be shared with the entire class, unless the instructor wants to use it in a different capacity. The learners can use the online journal to capture their thoughts about their service experience from visit to visit.

- **Sharing their learning with their instructor and classmates** (Internships, Practicums): vlogs, blogs, and online journals can also be used for learners completing internships and practicums to keep a recorded history of their experiences. Instructors can post weekly/bi-weekly prompts that learners need to answer and provide learners with a choice of where to house their experiences at their placement sites. These prompts can be connected to some of the areas of professionalism the learners were focusing on at their internships/ practicum sites, while connecting to the current or prior course content. Since the vlogs and online blogs will likely be uploaded to a public forum within the online course shell, learners in the course may recognize that they are having similar experiences at their respective sites, and offer support, ideas, and commiseration. The online journal can be used privately by the learner with access granted to the instructor for learners to document their struggles and growth areas they are making at their placement. Another way to use the online journal is to record questions that the learners may want to address at a later date with the instructors.

- **Documenting their experiences with visuals** (Study Abroad): Learners who are completing a study abroad experience as part of their online courses can take advantage of mobile technologies to document their experience and share with their instructors and classmates. Depending on the structure of the course, learners will all be in the same country, or in different countries throughout the world. For example, the course could be a public health course, where online learners complete a study abroad experience in a developing country in a public hospital or medical facility working with people on public health concerns.

Vlog, blog and online journal tools

Many learning management tools have features that would allow learners to create blogs and journals within the online course system. Some may even have a video capability to create vlogs (see Figure 2.4). Table 2.2 details some other options that can be introduced to learners for them to reflect on their service-learning experiences, share with their instructors their learning, and document their experiential learning experiences.

Figure 2.4 PocketVideo is an example of a vlogging application that can be used with mobile devices

Source: Image used with permission of Pocket Video

Table 2.2 Vlog, blog and online journal tools

Tool	Website	Short overview
PocketVideo	https://pocket.video	Create vlogs from a mobile device with the ability to add animations and music.
Lightt	https://lightt.com	The ability to create vlogs by combining separate segments into one finished product, with many editing and special effect features.
Voicethread	https://voicethread.com	Allows for the creation of vlogs using audio, video, and complementary text, with the option for the ability of having the instructor and classmates comment directly on the vlog, at any time.
WordPress	https://wordpress.com	This site allows for blog creation using attractive templates.
Penzu	https://penzu.com	Private journaling site that is password protected.
Journalate	https://journalate.com	Another option for journaling that provides privacy and attractive templates.

Video conferencing tools

The use of video conferencing tools to connect with learners in real-time when they are completing an experiential learning experience is critical in keeping the connection and guiding the learners' experiences. Video conferencing is different from web conferencing, as web conferencing is more of a one-way interaction. In a web conference, large amounts of data are typically shared to a large group of people. This format can be highly efficient and useful in large online lecture-based courses where the instructor needs to teach a substantial amount of content to learners, with no time to meet them individually. Since learners who are completing experiential learning activities would spend so much time out of the online course, video conferencing would be a more appropriate way for the instructors to connect with the learners and provide them with instruction, creating a two-way interaction experience. Video conferencing with learners can serve different purposes depending on the type of experiential learning experience the learners are completing; however, in general video conferencing can be used in the following ways:

- *Continuity in course content delivery*: One reason why it may be believed that it is not feasible to include experiential learning into an online course, is because there is seemingly no way to hold a class with all learners, or a seamless way to provide the course content that connects the experiential learning to learners who are in different cities, states and countries, completing their internships, practicums, service-learning and study abroad requirements. Video conferencing can be used to provide the course content to learners that connect to the experiences they are having while studying abroad, completing an internship, or participating in a practicum. Not only can course content be delivered through video conferencing, learners can ask questions and receive clarification that can impact their experiential learning experience.
- *Providing learners with feedback*: Video conferencing can also fill the void in not being able to physically meet with learners to guide their experiential learning experiences and provide them with feedback. Feedback is extremely important in any class, but particularly in online courses where learners may feel isolated. Establishing regular check-in video conferencing sessions with learners can assist with facilitating the experiential learning experience for learners, from a distance.
- *Meet with site supervisors and community organizations*: Meeting with the site supervisors and representatives from the different community organizations that learners are completing their experiential learning experience at is critical. Depending on the type of experiential learning activity it is, the amount of meetings will vary. For example, when setting up an internship, the instructor may want to meet at

the beginning of the course to go over the expectations of the experience. In a service-learning course, community organizations hosting learners may want to meet more regularly to reflect on how things are going. In a study abroad experience, the instructors may meet with a representative of an institution several months before the course is expected to begin to plan the in-country activities.

Scheduling video conferences in asynchronous online courses

Scheduling a mutually agreed upon time to video conference with your learners about their experiential learning experiences can be one of the most difficult aspects of organizing an experiential learning component into any online course. Similar to trying to meet colleagues, finding a common time with people with many other obligations can be quite challenging. There are several free options for web-based scheduling services. "Doodle" is a popular option particularly when seeking to schedule a meeting time for several people. As the instructor, you can select several time slots on different days that work for you, and create a doodle poll (see Figure 2.5).

Once the poll is created, a link is generated and can be sent to learners. If you would like to meet smaller groups of learners

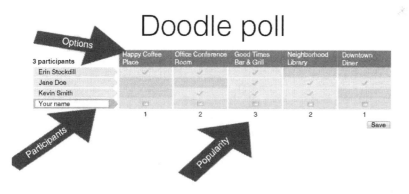

Figure 2.5 Doodle is a free web-based scheduling tool that can be used to schedule conference times with online learners

Source: Image used with permission of Doodle

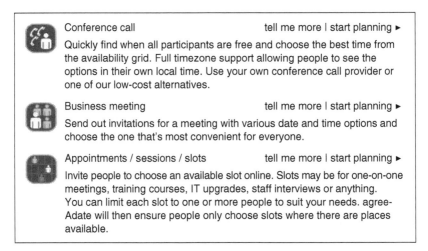

Conference call   tell me more | start planning ▸

Quickly find when all participants are free and choose the best time from the availability grid. Full timezone support allowing people to see the options in their own local time. Use your own conference call provider or one of our low-cost alternatives.

Business meeting   tell me more | start planning ▸

Send out invitations for a meeting with various date and time options and choose the one that's most convenient for everyone.

Appointments / sessions / slots   tell me more | start planning ▸

Invite people to choose an available slot online. Slots may be for one-on-one meetings, training courses, IT upgrades, staff interviews or anything. You can limit each slot to one or more people to suit your needs. agree-Adate will then ensure people only choose slots where there are places available.

Figure 2.6 agreeAdate.com is a free online meeting scheduler

Source: This image is being used with permission from agreeAdate

within the larger class, you will be able to visually identify times that each group member is available. Another option is "agreeAdate", which can be used to schedule individual meetings with learners (see Figure 2.6). One of the features that is useful for agreeAdate is the reminder feature; how often and when the learner is automatically reminded about their appointment is determined by the instructor making the appointments. Once appointments have been scheduled, the instructor may also want to post the schedule somewhere within the online course so the learners are always reminded of their upcoming video conference. Some examples of videoconferencing and scheduling tools are described in Table 2.3.

Instructor's Role in Organizing Experiential Learning in Online Courses

As an online instructor, it is your responsibility to assist learners with finding a suitable placement related to the type of experiential learning activity the learner will be involved in. This process will be different from what it would be if the learners and experiential learning sites were all located in an area close to campus, as it would be in a typical bricks and mortars course. Because students are

Table 2.3 Virtual conferencing and scheduling tools

Tool	Website	Key features
Zoom	https://www.zoom.us	Zoom is a robust option for video conferencing with free features such as screen sharing, annotating on a white board, and chat messaging.
Google Hangouts	https://hangouts.google.com	Another option for video conferencing through video and phone.
Fuze	https://www.fuze.com	Video conferencing including VOIP with free online tech support.
Doodle	https://doodle.com/	Scheduling tool with the ability to sync with Google and Outlook calendars when searching for a time.
Agreeadate	http://www.agreeadate.com	Scheduling tool that sends out reminders and allows for group scheduling or time slots.

geographically distant, as an instructor, you may not have any local contacts to rely on. The online instructor must determine a plan for receiving updates on the experience throughout the course and what tangible assignments will be required from the learners. Throughout the experience, the online instructor should connect course content to the experiences that the learners are having, and help learners to think critically about the experiences and application of them in the real world. It may be helpful to create Google Forms for various items of paperwork which at a minimum should include:

- Site Supervisor Contract/Commitment Form
- Learner Expectations, Description of the Experience, and Related Course Assignments
- Evaluation Form for Site Supervisors and Learners.

Resources for Coordinating Experiential Learning Placements

Depending on the institution, the level of involvement from instructors in terms of helping learners to coordinate their respective experiential learning experiences will differ. Many colleges and universities will work through offices such as career development, civic engagement, and their respective academic departments to assist learners with securing placements. If your course is more independent, with the greater responsibility given to the instructor and learner, not having local connections since the learners are scattered around the country and world, might present a challenge. Below we share a few websites and organizations to start with when looking for placements for learners. This list is in alphabetical order and is not exhaustive:

- American Association of Colleges of Pharmacy – AACP Advanced Pharmacy Practice Experience: http://www.aacp.org
- American Bar Association: http://www.americanbar.org/aba.html
- American Health Information Management Association (Professional Practice Experience (PPE): http://www.ahima.org/ppe
- American Nurses Association: http://www.nursingworld.org/default.aspx
- Association for Experiential Education: http://www.aee.org
- Association of International Education Administrators: http://www.aieaworld.orght
- Association for Teacher Educators: http://www.ate1.org/pubs/home.cfm
- Campus Compact: http://compact.org
- Cooperative Education and Internship Association: http://www.ceiainc.org
- Institute of International Education: http://www.iie.org
- International Association for Research on Service-Learning and Community Engagement: http://www.researchslce.org
- National Association of Colleges and Employers: http://www.naceweb.org/internships/
- National Association of International Educators: http://www.nafsa.org

- National Business Education Association: https://www.nbea.org
- National Education Association: http://www.nea.org/home/1600.htm
- National Society for Experiential Education: http://www.nsee.org
- WACE (Cooperative and Work-Integrated Education): http://www.waceinc.org

Summary

This chapter has provided you with an understanding of the many opportunities for experiential learning in the classroom. Different forms of experiential learning, including internships, cooperative education, practicums, study abroad, and service-learning were defined. In this chapter we also shared ideas for embedding an experiential learning opportunity into online courses, and explained how to connect specific types of experiential learning to various academic disciplines. Vlogs, virtual blogs, online journaling, video conferencing, mobile apps, tools with the LMS, and video and picture documentation tools are available that can connect experiential learning with course content, instructors and other learners. The next chapter will look at how to embed project-based and scenario-based learning into online courses.

3
Project- and Scenario-Based Learning

Introduction

When we think of project and scenario-based learning, learners have the opportunity to interact with the course content and help each other solve problems. One of the strongest historical proponents of this strategy was Lev Vygotsky, who pioneered the socio-cultural view of learning and development. According to Vygotsky what a learner can do with the assistance of others can influence or be even more indicative of their mental development than what a learner can do alone (Panofsky, 2003). Vygotsky's theory that learners can develop through the influence of culture (social interaction) and interpersonal communication refers to a person's knowledge for how to do something based on the social context. This type of learning environment provides the basis for which a learner's culturally or socially-shaped cognitive development is applied to real-world situations. Furthermore, the way the world appears to learners through project and scenario-based learning influences the culture's understanding of the world and how learners can use the appropriate tools to practice or demonstrate their learning. Multiple identities are formed by group participation in the culture and use of the tools. Educators have specifically described these two foundational learning approaches "as strong support for creating and sharing one's creations, and some type of informal mentorship whereby what is known by the most experienced is passed along to novices" (Jenkins et al., 2009, p. 29).

The idea is that project and scenario-based learning in the online classroom helps to shape the influence of social context among the learners within the learning environment. Particularly, Vygotsky (Panofsky, 2003) indicates that the role of the teacher, facilitator, peer, or another teaching device (i.e. computer, mobile, etc.) is critical to how learners learn. When learners are engaged in these types of activities, learning takes place. Today, we realize that modern technology provides an effective platform for teachers to maximize learning online. It follows that the "teaching devices" which Vygotsky mentions can be many forms of technology as well as how technology plays a major role in shaping a learner's identity by affecting the way that they learn.

Project Based Learning

The Buck Institute for Education (BIE) states that Project Based Learning (PBL) is a dynamic classroom approach in which learners actively explore real-world problems and challenges, and learners are inspired to obtain a deeper knowledge of the subjects they are studying (BIE, 2015). More specifically, it is through project-based learning where it is the role of the learner to investigate significant questions that require them to gather information and think critically. The core learning approach of PBL also allows the learner to learn through motivation, interest, and apply new knowledge in a problem-solving context (see Figure 3.1).

According to Barron and Darling-Hammond (2008), a project-based learning curricula includes:

- students gaining learning knowledge to tackle **realistic problems** as they would be solved in the real world;
- increased **learner control** over his or her learning;
- teachers serving as **coaches and facilitators** of inquiry and reflection;
- learners (usually, but not always) working in **pairs or groups**.

Figure 3.1 A graphical representation of the elements of project-based learning

Note: This image is being used with permission from Shutterstock, Inc.

On the other hand, the role of the instructor in PBL is that of the facilitator, who interacts with learners to help guide them to frame meaningful questions, organizing tasks, facilitating the conversation of knowledge development, as well as providing ongoing feedback on what learners have learned from their experiences (see Figure 3.2).

Buckingham (2006) also mentions the differences between the types of technologies that can shape PBL learning experiences. The two major categories are social technologies and cultural technologies. Social technologies are tools that organize social

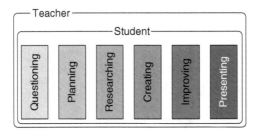

Figure 3.2 The teacher and learner model for project-based learning

activities within the learning environment. The primary focus of social technologies is on the group members. In today's online learning environments, examples would include participation in social media such as Instagram, Facebook, Twitter or group areas that are built in the LMS. Cultural technologies, on the other hand, are tools that organize processes for group communication and collaboration. Google Docs, YouTube and virtual worlds are examples of cultural technologies in which learners can be involved. When learners are engaged in these types of activities, the learning is mediated by the social positions and community contexts that organize participation, which forms an identity in that particular environment.

Since PBL can afford creative expression, role play, mentorship and apprenticeship, they have become high-traffic spaces for innovation and learning. This sounds ideal in the sense that every online course can incorporate a PBL assignment – where learners believe their contributions matter and they feel socially connected. However, educators cannot just change lesson plans to create such an environment; there must be entire shifts in the way educators teach. PBL is a unique learning approach because it creates an engulfing learning environment; something that old traditional classroom methods could not do. There needs to be some vehicle, which transports a classroom from the classic lecture to a more interactive and rich environment. That vehicle is PBL within the social-cultural context, of which Vygotsky was a huge proponent.

One of the benefits of PBL is that learners will have equal opportunity to the course material whether they are novices or masters of the information. In a way, this is an acting apprenticeship, where instructors take on the role of the facilitator in the learning environment and serve as a resource of knowledge for those learners not as familiar with the subject matter. PBL is also a great example of an affinity space that promotes intensive and extensive knowledge, individual and distributed knowledge, dispersed and tacit knowledge accompanied by various forms and routes of participation (Gee, 2004). In the online classroom, PBL can happen virtually, bringing together learners that may have never met. These connections open a whole new world to hands-on, collaborative learning and experiences.

Today's 21st-century learners are acquiring useful skills through PBL in these types of learning environments. In addition, this can be beneficial in how an individual's problem-solving skills can be used not only to facilitate learning, but also to assess learning outcomes, alternative methods for communication and abilities in the classroom. The impact of PBL on learning is vast and will continue to expand over the years. Active learning and continuous engagement are key to maintaining an understanding of the evolving relationship between PBL and learner mastery. Table 3.1 provides some examples of project-based learning.

Scenario-based learning

Evans and Taylor (2005) define scenario-based learning as "stories focused on a user or group of users, which would provide information on the nature of the users, the goals they want to achieve and the context in which the activities will take place" (Evans & Taylor, 2005, p. 8). Scenario-based learning (SBL) has a great advantage in the online course environment over traditional learning methods. It is widely accepted that learners tend to learn best when their learning is part of a "highly motivated engagement with social practices which they value" (Gee, 2004, p. 33). In fact, according to Jenkins et al. (2009), educators have always known that learners learn more

Table 3.1 Project-based learning examples

Learning activity	Description
Exploratory walks or site visits	Learners can participate in a site visit of a location such as their neighborhood, facility, or virtual quest. This activity can also involve scavenger hunts or local expeditions.
Using current events	Incorporating current news events around the world to learn more about a particular issue or problem.
Creative writing exercises (role playing)	Learners can work together to construct narrative stories or presentation based on their assigned roles.
Science experiments	Learners can conduct lab experiment and analyze their findings.
Using data and math	Scheduling tool that sends out reminders and allows for group scheduling or time slots.
Debates (oral presentation)	Learners can collaborate to discuss court cases or research topics of interests which would have them choose a "side/stance" where each learner must provide their rationale and explanations to support their arguments.

through direct observation and experimentation than from reading about something in a textbook or listening to a lecture.

Sorin et al. (2012) have outlined five types of scenarios that can be implemented in the classroom. Note that every type of scenario is suited for teaching a particular type of skill and that instructors would have to decide which type of scenario would be the most effective based on the course materials. Here are the major types of scenarios:

- **Skill-Based Scenario:** In this scenario, the learner is expected to demonstrate skills and knowledge that have already been acquired.
- **Problem-Based Scenario:** This type of scenario is ideal for situations where learners have to integrate their theoretical and practical knowledge to investigate a problem. Decision-making, logical reasoning, and critical analyses are integral components of these scenarios.

- **Issue-Based Scenario:** In this type of a scenario, learners get to take a stand on issues, usually with humanitarian perspectives, and explore these to understand how these affect decision-making in professional spheres.
- **Speculative Scenario:** In this scenario, learners have to predict the outcome of an event in the future based on their knowledge and deductions.
- **Gaming Scenario:** This type of scenario involves the use of games as learning tools.

SBL is considered to be a great teaching tool for an active learner. SBL presents learners with the opportunity to learn through the direct experience by playing a role or becoming a character and infusing oneself into a virtual situation. Being able to "see the problem in a particular context" affords the learner an increased understanding for using the new knowledge (Brown, Collins & Duguid, 1989, p. 39), as can be seen in Figure 3.3.

SBL can have a myriad of playful activities and basic exchanges that relay skills, knowledge and information and can be viewed as

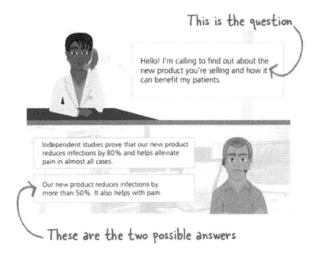

Figure 3.3 Articulate Storyline is a tool that allows you to create web-based scenarios

a tool by which the learner can select and determine the medium (affiliation) or method (learning tool) that is best suited for them.

A benefit of SBL is that it allows learners to apply their content knowledge and problem-solving skills to explore new or complex situations that support the learning outcomes. It also provides learners with the opportunity to reinforce learning concepts in a way that learners can always go back and practice their skills using motivation as a guide to make the appropriate decisions to get to the "correct" answer. Finally, creating SBL for the classroom environment can add value to the learning experience. In online learning environments, learners have the opportunity to share and apply their understandings of the subject matter. This form of scenario-based learning enhances the learners' learning abilities and ensures that the learners are being challenged appropriately when finding solutions as well-informed citizens of society. One limitation to using the scenario-based approach is that it involves a huge amount of time from both the teacher and designer. The teacher must be very intentional about the content and provide narrative feedback at every level to scaffold the learning. Figure 3.4 outlines the various types of content and level of instructor feedback that are needed to support course material using the SBL approach.

In this respect, SBL's plethora of options for interaction and information sharing is reshaping the landscape for online learning and its learners. Thus, scenario-based learning must be balanced with the scenario's challenges (skills that you expect the learners to gain or develop) with the problems (action activities) that need solving to determine learner mastery or comprehension.

SBL resources

See the following websites for some SBL resources:

- www.articulate.com/rapid-elearning/build-branched-e-learning-scenarios-in-three-simple-steps/
- www.mindomo.com

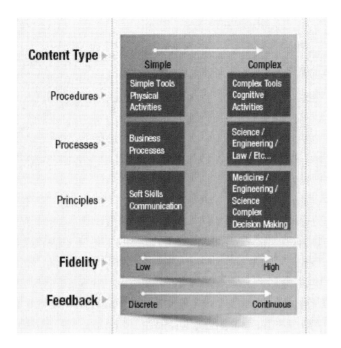

Figure 3.4 Upside learning

- www.mindjet.com
- www.sblinteractive.org/
- http://pbl.massey.ac.nz/pbl-interactive-public-scenarios.htm

The Role of Motivation in Learning

Psychology has made major contributions in helping people to understand how an individual learns. Based on psychology research, motivation or interest can be classified in the Self Determination learning theory. As an instructional approach, the Self Determination Theory (SDT) supports the learning environment in a way that it helps to differentiate between the various types of motivation that can lead to a particular action or response (Ryan & Deci, 2000). This is essential for learning because educators can understand the importance of fostering an environment that promotes active participation from learners and allows them to take responsibility for their own learning. According to Ryan and Deci (2000), motivation involves energy, direction, and persistence – all aspects of activation and intention. Motivation invokes a particular response to a certain task. Individuals are stimulated to act by different factors. They can be motivated because they value an activity or even simply wanting to please others. A major focus of SDT has been to understand motivation as being exhibited at any given time. SDT has been able to identify distinct types of motivation, such as intrinsic and extrinsic, both of which have played a key role in learning and performance.

Intrinsic motivation. Ryan and Deci (2000) define intrinsic motivation as the *doing* of an activity for inherent satisfaction rather than for some separable consequence. Learners that are intrinsically motivated are moved to act for the enjoyment or pleasure that it entails. In other words, intrinsic motivation naturally exists within individuals. People tend to be motivated to some activities and not others. This is a crucial element in the learning environment because it is through this type of motivation that learners will act on their interests so that they can develop knowledge and skills for the subject matter.

One example that educators can use to promote intrinsic motivation in the classroom using project- and scenario-based learning is to involve learners in choice learning activities. PBL and SBL can facilitate choices in learning and have the ability to offer feedback about the effectiveness of the choice being made. For example, learners can be given a choice of what to do (role, approach, tasks, etc.) for SBL assignments. This learner choice increases feelings of self determination, interest and engagement. Allowing learners to choose learning activities which they are familiar with encourages active participation, creativity and improves problem-solving skills. Furthermore, choice in SBL gives learners a greater sense of responsibility which in turn, increases the motivation to learn.

Extrinsic motivation. The second type of motivation is extrinsic motivation. Extrinsic motivation happens whenever the activity is done in order to attain some separable outcome or for instrumental value, rather than that one may find it interesting (Ryan

& Deci, 2000). A typical example of extrinsic motivation can be seen in PBL where learners are working together to achieve a particular goal or task. The most useful thing is that learners get to see how the decisions they make affect others by using real-life situations. This form of extrinsic motivation plays an imperative role in the learning process that focuses on decision-making skills and communication skills that can lead to greater persistence to internalize, apply and understand the content material.

Motivation, whether intrinsic or extrinsic, can increase learning and engagement through the use of PBL and SBL learning activities. For example, teachers can refer to what Nakamura and Csikszentmihalyi (2002) describe as flow theory in which motivation occurs when there is a balance between the learner's skills and the challenges they face with the content or activity. In order for the learner to stay motivated, the challenge or the learning activity has to increase as the learner's skills increase. The area of perfect balance between skills and challenge is called the "flow channel" (see Figure 3.5) (Nakamura & Csikszentmihalyi, 2002), which is known as the state of maximal motivation in which the learner is truly engaged and highly motivated to solve a problem.

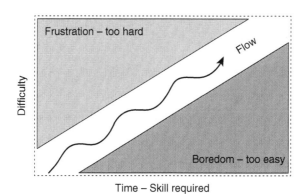

Figure 3.5 The flow channel

Summary

In conclusion, project-based and scenario-based learning can help with supporting the learner, providing helpful activities that are designed to enhance their learning. They can help learners understand what is relevant to the learning activity before having to complete the assignment. PBL and SBL tend to focus on certain topics and information for learning, as well as encouraging learners to be active learners. These types of learning experiences give learners the freedom to participate in areas that interest them or things they want to learn about. Learners can try things without fear of being wrong, promoting innovation, and have the capability of adopting different perspectives and discovering new things. Finally, a major key attribute of PBL and SBL culture is networking where learners connect with others in the online class environment (e.g. teacher and their peers) and are also able to interpret, share knowledge and construct real-world cases. In the next chapter we will focus on how gamification and social media tools can be implemented in the online learning environment.

4

Gamification and Social Media

Educators cannot just change lesson plans to create such an environment; there must be entire shifts in the way educators teach. Gamification and social media are unique because they create an engulfing learning environment; something that old classroom methods could not do. There needs to be some vehicle, which transports a classroom from the classic lecture to a more interactive and rich environment. Gaming and play are considered great teaching tools for an active learner (see Figure 4.1). Digital gaming, a means of participatory culture, presents the opportunity to learn through the direct experience of playing a role or becoming a character and infusing oneself into a virtual situation. Being able to "see the problem in a particular context" affords the learner an increased understanding for using the new knowledge (Brown et al., 1989, p. 35).

One particularly intriguing technology-based platform involves game-based learning, in which individuals play games in different ways, using different gaming strategies and decision-making skills. Game-based learning not only cultivates learner development, but also enhances skills needed in education; such as trouble-shooting, trial and error, team building skills, problem solving, lateral thinking, concentration, memorization, information gathering, analysis, developing and testing solutions (Gros, 2007). Game-based learning is most prevalent in the K-12 environment (covering both primary and secondary schools), where the value of teaching learners in a risk-free environment provides

Figure 4.1 This is a visual representation of how games can be used as a learning tool

Source: Image used with permission of Shutterstock, Inc.

an interactive atmosphere that incorporates all of the design elements in which learners can interact with games in a meaningful way (Hew & Brush, 2007). However, there are not many higher education institutions today that have engaged in quality game-based learning for undergraduate and professional learners that are in distance learning programs – which may be due to budget constraints and lengthy course development factors. However, there is a potential role for game-based learning "variables" or limitations to improve a distance education's technology plan that caters to this learner demographic (Chee, 2007).

Game-based research is used to study learning environments, which are designed and systematically changed by the researcher (Squire, 2006). We believe that utilizing game-based learning to analyze and understand a particular learning concept is beneficial not only to obtain results but also because it provides the ability to modify the curriculum and to understand how game-based learning can enhance the learning environment for learners.

The Psychology of Play and Learning

The concept of play, particularly in the context of learning, is complex and multifaceted, but a commonly accepted definition is "free movement" (Vygotsky, 1979, para. IV) which relates directly to learning in that learners can learn in different ways based on their intellect, developmental level, and past experiences. However, the learning process is constrained by rigid structures such as the "correct" answers and processes for the subject.

Play has always been considered a source of learning and can be used as a vehicle to communicate how new knowledge and ideas can be transferred in the classroom. Early philosophers, like Plato, believed that "play in childhood is preparation for future career" (Huang & Plass, 2009). Therefore, seeing that play is an already accepted mechanism for learning and recognizing that play exists in many forms of participatory culture gives rise to the notion that participatory culture is shaping the development of learning. Yet, the real learning challenge lies in connecting knowledge with decisions in the context of our everyday situations (Jenkins et al., 2009).

Play as a learning tool can be implemented in the learning environment. In game play, rules can be established to govern the learning content, but the learners would be free to learn differently. Through ludic activities, learners are engaged by the end-goal of learning something, although exact rules for achieving this goal are not established. In both of these examples we see that play can be transformative. In fact, transformative play, in the context of learning, is optimal for maximizing the zone of proximal development, as outlined by Vygotsky (1979). This is because changing the rigid structure of play in response to the participants' progress would effectively change the potential for effective interaction with the environment and instructors. A fitting example of this would be a computer adaptive learning tool that alters the learning framework based on the learners' previous answers. Maximizing learning for the learner would require the tool to recognize a pattern of answering and to develop an assistance module to effectively aid the user when answering subsequent questions.

Using games and simulated virtual worlds to explore is yet another way that participatory culture is shaping the evolution of a new learning landscape. Designing avatars or online characters in virtual worlds causes users to experiment with alternate identities or projective selves (Gee, 2003). These roles or "personas they assume in the game" (Jenkins et al., 2009, p. 47) represent different options for identities not only in the virtual world, but also in the real world. Without challenging the ethical position of identity experimentation in the gaming world, let it suffice to say that participatory culture exposes its users to multiple choices for self-identity which is necessarily a process in self-reflection and a valuable exercise in both social and work situations that generally leads to increased learning and understanding of a particular event.

Klopfer (2008) defines games as "purposeful, goal-orientated, rule-based activity that the players perceive as fun" (p. 11). Games are great tools for learning content because they create authentic opportunities for 21st-century learners to build on previous knowledge and develop in-depth knowledge and skills. Games are highly engaging, interactive, and in order for a game to be effective in the learning environment it must be used effectively. Today's online learners desire interactive learning experiences and it is vital that through research, educators explore the possibilities of using emerging digital media technologies like games in the learning environment.

Game Play Styles and Player Types

Game researchers believe that player styles can be viewed as fluid. Users tend to move from one play style to another and engage in a wide variety of play styles at various times, and in different contexts. The five player types of learning games classified by the studies of Richard Bartle (2004) and Nick Yee (2004) include: Achiever, Explorer, Careless, Lost and Self-Validator. Achievers play games quickly and naturally focus on doing well or finding ways to achieve mastery. Explorers are slow players that tend to enjoy game mechanics rather than following game guidelines. Careless players play quickly, but tend to make mistakes while doing so. Lost players, like Explorers, play games slowly; however, they make many errors and tend not to enjoy the gaming experience. Finally, Self-Validators are players that do not like failing. They desire easy game play with levels that are not challenging, easy to navigate and have the ability to quickly receive high scores. In learning games, Self-Validators worry about failing which leads to an interference with the learning process. Based on Heeter's (2009) definition of player types, Careless and Lost are considered ineffective learning styles which could be due to their lack of motivation to play games well while making numerous (and repeated) mistakes. In this chapter, we will briefly review the player types of Achiever, Explorer and Self-Validator as examples of successful learning styles for game play.

Achievers. Achievers require strict goals and increasing challenges. They would strive on playing games that offer specific point goals and performance measurements. Achievers thrive on goal-specific constraints that require overcoming obstacles, which in turn, offers them some sort of in-game reward. The game, Food Force, could be considered a game that Achievers would enjoy. In this particular game, players must complete six missions, in which they are tasked with assessing hunger, determining nutritional needs, buying and distributing supplies in order to help a country during a hunger crisis.

Explorers. Explorers do not necessarily need challenges during game play. If challenges are included, they should revolve around in-depth game content. Explorers enjoy testing hypotheses and studying the game-world through customization and free access to more game content. A sandbox game like Minecraft would be a preferred game choice for Explorers. Sandbox games allow players to roam freely through a virtual world. Players are not limited to invisible barriers or loading screens like other genres of games. Minecraft allows a broad range of ways to reach an objective and focuses on player creativity and construction. Players must build structures out of textured blocks in a virtual three-dimensional world, while surviving enemies and overcoming obstacles. Serious game styles can also add content and depth to interest Explorers and encourage players to experience intrinsic rewards from playing and learning (Heeter, 2009).

Self-Validators. Self-Validators require easier challenges where the game adapts to the skills a player is fond of and rewards players implicitly as they make progress through the game (Heeter, Magerko, Medler & Fitzgerald, 2009). Self-Validators also need games that offer them game play hints and clues, provide practice sessions, avoid negative feedback and allow them to hide bad performances. A game like Grand Theft Auto would suit the needs of a Self-Validator player type. Here, the player is free to do whatever he or she wants. More, specifically, Grand Theft Auto allows a player to gain points based on performing tasks successfully. A successful completion rewards the player with points and opens the opportunity to complete other tasks to get even higher rewards.

Motivation, Learning and Player Types

Intrinsic and extrinsic motivations in games have implications for play styles and learning. Play styles coupled with motivation are what ultimately drive players to choose their game strategy. Achievers are motivated by extrinsic achievement goals like winning and approval. Explorers are motivated by intrinsic goals, taking an interest in the content of games. They also enjoy exploring ideas, role-playing, and game mechanics more than earning top scores (Heeter, 2009). Self-Validators appear to be motivated by rewards, such as achieving the highest score, and desire easy game successes.

Players gain competence through trial, error and feedback. Self-Validators are more likely to play learning games than entertainment games. Learning games offer these players success that is often linked to intelligence, ability and real-world advancement. Teachers can monitor in-game learner achievement while utilizing learning games. Game designers create learning games that often offer less negative feedback in order to cater to the Self-Validator players. Feedback that focuses on player performance can help push Self-Validators towards a mastery orientation.

Role of Motivation in Game Play

Motivation, whether intrinsic or extrinsic, can increase learning and engagement through the use of games. Games can facilitate choices in learning and have the ability to offer feedback about the effectiveness of the choice being made. In one particular game, CyberBully Avenger, players are presented with scenarios about cyber bullying and they have to make decisions about what to do. The most useful thing is that players get to see how the decisions they make affect others in the game by using real-life situations.

Secondly, games can help with supporting the learner, providing helpful cues to enhance self-directed learning. Games can be used to help learners understand what is relevant to the learning activity before having to complete the assignment. Games tend to focus on certain topics and information for learning. They can encourage learners to be active learners.

Learners do their best work when engaged in activities such as educational games that are personally meaningful to them (Ryan & Deci, 2000). An example of how games can be used to increase motivation and active participation is through the use of virtual environments, such as Second Life. In this application, learners are avatars that can interact with one another. Educators can allow learners to meet virtually, create learning activities that allow the learners to explore the virtual world in real time (Dede, 2007). It is through this virtual environment that instructors can promote a different learning perspective that evaluates learner performance, monitors the interaction between classmates (peer learning), and fosters intellectual discussions or reflections online.

Implications for Game Design and Curriculum Design

Instructional design and game design deal with motivation, challenge, individual differences and social interaction. Learning outcomes and goals set by teachers are closely related to the goals presented in digital games. Just as different players play games in different ways, different learners learn in different ways. Learning styles influence curriculum design, just as play styles influence game design. Game designers create digital games catered towards player needs and interests. For the most part, game designers try to accommodate one player type.

> Game designers who want to accommodate both Achievers and Explorers can try to include something for everyone, but sometimes Achievers' and Explorers' needs are incompatible, forcing design choices that privilege one or the other form of preferred play.
>
> (Heeter et al., 2009, p. 7)

Game designers must consider the player types and learning styles they want to accommodate and encourage in their game and design games accordingly. The game designer will try to focus on pleasing a certain player type and learning style, rather than trying to please them all.

Educators create instructional strategies based on learner needs and interests. Learner motivation also plays a huge role in education. Teachers utilize learner motivation, both extrinsic and intrinsic, in the classroom. When using educational games in the classroom, teachers must consider not only the content and orientation of a game, but also, the individual characteristics like motivation of the learners, or in this case the player types. Characteristics like motivation, competition, social interaction and learning styles must be evaluated prior to introducing games in the classroom. Motivational principles for empowering learners include the "ability to grant power, autonomy, and challenge at a player's level and implications for learners' identity" (Foster & Mishra, 2011, p. 37). The learning style of learners details learner strengths and weaknesses, which must be understood when incorporating not only games in the curriculum, but also any instructional approach. According to Heeter (2009), "because educational games have learning as well as entertainment goals, learning game player types need to incorporate player-learner characteristics such as learning styles, abilities, and achievement orientation" (p. 3).

Digital games not only cultivate learner development, but also enhance skills needed in education, like trouble-shooting, trial and error, team building skills, problem solving, lateral thinking, concentration, memorization, information gathering, analysis, developing and testing solutions. Characteristics of digital games, like competition, challenge, exploration, fantasy, goals, interaction, outcomes, people, rules, and safety, relate to the educational process. Learners can develop a deeper comprehension of content by using trouble-shooting and problem-solving skills while playing games (Wagner, 2012). In conclusion, motivation, whether intrinsic or extrinsic, can increase learning and engagement through the use of games in the classroom. Thus, when games are closely tied to desired learning outcomes, learners are able to transform practical experiences into the classroom environment.

Implementing Games in the Online Learning Environment

Game-based learning applications, coupled with e-learning platforms, have created many possibilities for sharing and transferring knowledge and information to learners. This provides a potentially large cohort with games and simulation technologies that can be used more for engaging and supporting practices, as well as moving learning into informal domains, including knowledge management and performance support. Gaming applications that integrate learning and technology foster communication, problem-solving, and critical thinking skills and can be used especially in the distance environment to meet the required learning performance goals and standards.

Games are great tools for learning content because they create authentic opportunities for 21st-century learners to build on previous knowledge and develop in-depth knowledge and skills. It is through gamification that the motivational power of games can be applied to real-world problems such as, in our case, the motivational problems of schools. Motivation and engagement are major challenges for the American educational system (Bridgeland, Dilulio & Morison, 2006). American schools also face a shockingly high dropout rate: approximately 1.2 million learners fail to graduate from high school each year (All4Ed, 2010). Understanding the role of gamification in education, therefore, means understanding under what circumstances game elements can drive learning behavior. Making use of Salen and Zimmerman's Rules, Play, and Culture framework (2003), we can better break down the impact of gamification. Gamification can change the rules, but it can also affect learners' emotional experiences, their sense of identity and their social positioning. Thus, this game-based approach to learning is supported by Leblanc's (2004) intrinsic motivation theory in which learners can change their identities as learners based on how motivated they are to learning the content.

Tools for Gaming

During your course, you may decide to use gaming as a way to actively engage your learners in the course. In addition to using gaming to engage learners, you can also develop summative assessments that look at certain skills of the learners, depending on the course. Table 4.1 provides some examples of games that have been implemented into the learning environment.

Table 4.1 Examples of games that have been implemented in the learning environment

Discipline	Game type	Learning goal(s)
Architecture, Design, and Animation	Minecraft (https://minecraft.net)	Learners will be able to practice vital skills related to the subject-area, and produce a final product that can be used to assess their mastery.
Information Technology	Code Spell (http://codespells.org)	Learners can practice their coding skills, and the instructor can assess their process and final product.
History and Politics	iCivics (https://www.icivics.org/games)	Learners are given different civic roles which allows them to address real-world issues.
Mathematics	Dreambox Learning (http://www.dreambox.com/k-8-math-lessons)	Learners can practice math skills using games.
Social Science	Food Force (http://www.download-free-games.com/freeware_games/food_force.htm)	Learners can complete missions to help end world hunger. Basic skills include identifying the community and land areas, air assessment, and then must strategize a plan to resolve hunger issues.
Science	Quest Atlantis Remixed (http://atlantisremixed.org/)	Learners can complete certain quests in a community-based virtual environment.
Engineering	Design a Parachute (http://tryengineering.org/play-games)	Learners are provided with the specific requirements and data in order to design test their prototype.

The Role of Social Media in Learning

Learning in the 21st century now requires classrooms to be more participatory and collaborative, allowing learners to use social media technologies to network and to transfer material. And communication has allowed learners of differing perspectives to enter into a social platform where every learner has a voice, where learners have a learning community where:

- They believe that their contributions to the content matter.
- They feel more socially connected with one another and the instructor.
- They appreciate the feedback and responses they receive that shapes their learning perspectives and perceptions.

Figure 4.2 A graphical representation of the types of social media applications used for learning

Source: Image used with permission of Shutterstock, Inc.

Cognitive development through participatory culture has a great advantage over traditional learning methods. Since around 2012, social media has been widely accepted by educators. Gee (2004) mentioned that "people learn best when their learning is part of a highly motivated engagement with social practices which they value" (p. 77). In fact, according to Jenkins et al. (2009), "educators have always known that learners learn more through direct observation and experimentation than from reading about something in a textbook or listening to a lecture" (p. 25). When social media tools are effectively incorporated into the learning environment, learners tend to be more engaged – this is a true example of learning mediated by the social positions and community contexts.

Table 4.2 provides some examples of social media tools that have been implemented in the learning environment.

Table 4.2 Some examples of social media tools that have been implemented in the learning environment

Types of social media tools	Learning outcomes
Twitter	A tool that allow learners to interact and share ideas, post images, and communicate with each other in real time.
Instagram	An image capturing tool that learners can use to showcase their projects/sample work as well as post images from a city or local exploration.
Piazza	An online discussion area where learners can post questions and answers in real time. Mostly computer science and engineering learners like this tool because it includes LaTeX editor to allow coding and computations.
Pinterest	A bookmarking tool that allows learners to create and document their ideas visually using images/graphics.
YouTube	A tool that allows learners to create, post, and watch video presentation and provide feedback.

Summary

Implementing gamification and social media in higher education is changing how courses are being designed and developed, especially with the rise in the use of mobile technologies. Today, learners more than ever have the opportunity to engage not only with the course material (within the classroom environment) but they are also able to create, collaborate, and articulate their practical experiences (outside the classroom environment). In this form of active learning, the roles of the instructor and student can be defined as either *learning designers or players* in which they are tasked to use game-based elements and social media to make decisions on how to use the course materials to demonstrate their learning in meaningful ways. In the next chapter, we will focus on the benefits and challenges of building social presence and participatory learning opportunities in online courses.

5
Building Social Presence Through Participatory and Peer-Learning Opportunities

Peer and Cooperative Learning in Online Courses

Benefits

There are many benefits for both learners and instructors when engagement in team projects is a requirement of the course. The opportunity to work with other classmates closely on an assignment provides the chance to learn a great deal from others. It is important to always actively engage online learners in the course content. Team projects inherently bring a social aspect to the forefront. There will be opportunities for team meetings, sharing, and time to contribute to the overall project which will make learners feel more connected to others in the online course. For online instructors, having to grade five team projects versus twenty individual projects also has its advantages. The instructor can spend the same amount of time that they would to grade individual assignments; however, more detailed feedback can be given since the instructor would have more time and energy. Another benefit of team projects in online courses is that larger projects become manageable since the workload is shared. This is particularly true for online courses that are accelerated, running in less weeks than traditional semester bricks and mortar courses.

Challenges

While there are many benefits to peer learning, there can be some that are challenging. Some of these challenges are particularly inherent in online courses. It is important in online courses for the instructor to design and facilitate team projects in a way that minimizes potential challenges that come with online team work including team conflicts and grading equity. In this chapter, we provide suggestions for building teams that take into account different personalities and work styles, as well as suggestions for grading team projects.

Social Presence

In order to actively engage learners in online courses, there must be opportunities for interactions with others. While there is something special about connecting with the course content and instructor, opportunities to reflect on learning and share the process with other individuals are also invaluable. The idea of social presence is part of the Community of Inquiry Framework developed by Rourke, Anderson, Garrison and Archer (2001). In the research done on social presence, three categories were focused on: affective, interactive and cohesive, which relate to emotions and immediacy, being present and extending learning, and inclusivity and connectedness of the class as a whole. Building social presence in online courses should be at the forefront and serve as a catalyst to creating targeted opportunities for learners to address course content through active engagement and team projects.

Designing Team Projects in Online Courses

Participating in team projects offers learners the chance to develop interpersonal communication skills (Figueira & Leal, 2013), build relationships with classmates, and increase the level of collective competencies as each group member brings something different to the team. However, in the online environment where the majority of the work occurs asynchronously, learners may resist having to work with others (Smith et al., 2011) on graded assignments. Learners often say that they do not like team assignments because they expect that they will have to contribute more than their teammates or that they will have difficulty scheduling times to meet other team members. They also may be uneasy about being assigned an individual grade based on the work of the team.

Online Instructor's Role in Designing Team Project

Create a virtual team space

All learning management systems (LMS) have tools and applications that serve teamwork well. Instructors should create a private virtual space for each team where team members can connect with one another and share ideas. At a minimum, the shared virtual team space should include a discussion board, a file sharing area, and a space for live, real-time sessions or chat. Instructors should provide an overview of each feature of the virtual shared space and make suggestions for how it should be used. While this may seem intuitive for instructors, some learners may not know how to best leverage the space or use the individual features. This can lead to underutilization of the shared virtual space and a less efficient process during the team project. Be sure that all learners know how to access and use the virtual team space to support the team's work.

Facilitate group dynamics

Do not wait for learners to email you when issues arise. Make it known that you will be "present" within the virtual space, and consistently offer advice and feedback as the team progresses through the project. It is important to do this in a manner that is not overly intrusive. You are simply guiding the process and making adjustments as needed if the team requires individualized support. This is also helpful for teams who are not able to transparently navigate the process and communicate their needs. Monitoring of the online team space also builds instructor presence within the online course and presents another opportunity to engage with learners virtually.

Set transparent expectations for individual contributions

Most assignments have general directions with a rubric explaining how the final product will be assessed. For team projects, it is imperative to go beyond this and identify individual contributions and expectations for each team member. A jigsaw approach could be employed in which the instructor divides the project into equal parts for each team member so all members know exactly what they are expected to do. If the instructor wants each team member to contribute something to the entire project, those expectations should be laid out with a framework to help facilitate that dissemination process.

Assign individual and team grades

It is important to assign both individual and team grades for the team assignments. Learners should be assessed on the individual contributions they made as well as on how well they participate in the team components. Assigning individual grades requires a clear expectation for individual contributions and progress monitoring throughout the project. Assigning individual grades increases individual accountability and can make for a more positive collaborative experience.

Develop a peer feedback system

The ability to provide and accept constructive feedback is part of being an adult. While this can be difficult and uncomfortable, it is an important part of the team project experience. In online courses especially, develop a template for peer feedback and share it with learners prior to the project. The constructs on the template can be based on key interpersonal skills that you are expecting learners to exhibit throughout the team project. Peer evaluations benefit learners who make contributions (Dingel & Wei, 2014), and can help address learners who do not fully participate in the collaborative experience. The knowledge that they will be evaluated by peers can motivate learners to work more collaboratively with their team members.

Intentionally create teams

The best teams are formed when each member can bring something different to the team. Having three leaders may cause tension, as there would be no one willing to be led. At the same time, if there are no leaders present, it may be difficult for the team to form a vision for the project and get the work started. Get to know your online learners and their preferences. This can come from a survey or preference inventory or through online discussion boards or other interactive course features. In a traditional class, you would see who the learners are sitting next to and engaging with; do the same within the online class. Are there certain people who always respond to each other's discussion board responses? Have you noticed that some people work at the same organization? Get to know your learners as much as possible within the online course, and be very intentional in creating teams.

Using preference inventories

One way to ensure that learners are paired with peers who they would work best with is to use preference inventories. For example, the Myers-Briggs personality inventory can be used to determine which learners would be more prone to lead the group versus those who may prefer to take a non-leading role. An online instructor can also create their own preference inventories and give it to learners at the beginning of the class. This would also help online instructors to get to know their learners better from the start of the class. Some of the questions on the preference inventory could be:

1. What city/country do you live in?
2. What time zone are you in?
3. Do you prefer to get class work completed in the mornings/evenings? Weekends/weekdays?
4. What type of roles do you feel comfortable taking in team projects?
5. What type of computer system do you use?

Random selection

Within most Learning Management Systems (LMS), there is a feature to create random teams. If the LMS you are using does not have this feature, a free random group selector such as RandomList (https://www.randomlists.com) can be used to randomly create teams.

Keep teams small and odd

Every learner is very busy with professional and personal obligations, making scheduling to meet as a team difficult. One of the most attractive features of online courses for learners is the ability to learn at times most convenient for the individual, without the requirement of being in class at certain times and days each week. The larger the teams, the more complicated scheduling can be. Teams, particularly in online courses where there are no regularly scheduled meetings, should be capped at approximately three learners. Having an odd number also eliminates the potential of teams being split when forced to make a decision. It is recommended that you encourage teams to come to a unanimous decision, but this may not always be possible. Having an odd number guarantees that there will always be a majority in the event of a team vote. There will be times when, because of the overall number of learners in the class, one group may need to consist of more than three learners, but in general, a team of three is more manageable and conducive to best practices in online teamwork.

Digital Tools for Collaboration

There are many tools that online instructors can encourage learners to leverage during collaborative projects. Many of these tools can be used to communicate with one another about the course projects, sharing and creating files and documents, and jointly present the final project online.

Communicating

Collaborative work with peers requires effective communication. There are many ways to communicate with each other in an online course including text and audio. Text communication in online courses typically occurs on a discussion board.

If the LMS your school is using does not have a conferencing tool for team projects, there are many options to use. In Chapter 2, we reviewed a few options including Google Hangouts. For peer and team projects, we recommend using Zoom HD as it allows for team members to share their screens with each other and also has an interactive whiteboard. Some of the other features of Zoom include sending invitations to join the meeting, screensharing abilities to record the session, and having private discussions within the large team. Team members can log into Zoom using a link or code, and can use their computers, tablets or mobile devices. Here are some ways to encourage teams to use virtual conferencing tools for collaboration:

- Require teams to have a planning meeting.
- Incorporate a team meeting in the grading process and have them submit a recording of a session.
- Require teams to have a post-assignment meeting and acknowledge what went well and areas of improvements.
- Meet the teams to discuss their progress on the assignment.
- Meet individual team members to give them a voice in the process.
- Have the team meet and use the screensharing features to show examples of other projects.

In addition to communicating during scheduled meetings, it is important to provide each team with other suggestions for keeping the lines of communication open. Have the learners determine which time zones everyone lives in, as well as which times generally work for each person to have discussions. Ask learners to post some sort of schedule within the LMS. Also encourage them to use email to send asynchronous messages that do not require the coordination of schedules. If learners would like to have a more personal element to the emails, they can be encouraged to use EyeJot (http://corp.eyejot.com) where their emails are turned into multimedia videos.

Creating, sharing and storing materials

One of the most important aspects of truly working together on the same project is the ability to be able to share ideas and thoughts. We recommend learners use Google Docs or similar tools, where one document can be viewed and edited by multiple people at the same time. The documents created on Google docs can also be downloaded as PDFs and Word documents, and shared with the instructor. To ensure that teams fully utilize shared documents, online instructors should provide clear and direct instructions on using the features of Google docs. Google itself has provided written and short video directions on the different features of Google docs. Some of the links have been provided below:

- Overview of Google Docs: https://support.google.com/docs/answer/49008?hl=en
- Google Doc in Plain English: https://www.youtube.com/watch?v=eRqUE6IHTEA
- Sharing in Google Docs: https://www.youtube.com/watch?v=POIR37Hmydg
- Discussions in Google Docs: https://www.youtube.com/watch?v=7zmOYziFKZw

To share and store materials outside of the Google drive system, most Learning Management Systems (LMS) such as Blackboard, have a file exchange feature. With the file exchange placed in a group space, teams will have access to it as well as the assignment description and other related materials.

Presenting

Depending on the type of project your online learners are actively engaged with, there may be a requirement to record a presentation that can be viewed by classmates and the instructor. Ideally, they have used the tools previously mentioned to create their presentation materials, but for the actual presentation, we suggest using Knovio (http://www.knovio.com) or Voicethread (https://voicethread.com). With Knovio, learners can upload the PowerPoint (.PPT) file that they worked on together in Google Slides, and record over them.

Knovio has the ability to record one slide at a time, at different times. For example, perhaps two team members can only record in the morning and one can record in the evening – Knovio allows for such a recording pattern. Knovio also allows the learners to create notes that they can read from, for the benefit of learners who are not as confident in their presentation and recording abilities. Slides within Knovio can be deleted and recorded over until the team is satisfied. Once completed, the presentation can be shared via a link that can be embedded within the online course shell.

Voicethread is another option online learners can use to present materials they have collaboratively worked on. Similarly to Knovio, teams will be able to upload slides they have already created into Voicethread. In addition to slides, images and video can also be uploaded into Voicethread. Once the presentation materials have been uploaded into Voicethread, each team member can record their voices on the different slides. Team members have the choice to record their voice only using the audio record feature, their voice and face using the video recorder feature, or just text by typing what they would like to say. In addition to recording on the computer, team members can call in using a telephone to do the recording. While presenting, if team members would like to highlight something, there is a doodling feature that allows them to collaboratively work together.

Examples of Peer-Learning Assignments in Online Courses

Regardless of the academic discipline, there are some types of assignments that lend themselves to peer learning, while other types of assignments are better suited to individuals. JigSaw, Accountability Teams, Case Studies, and Robust creative works can be part of any online course as a means to engage learners with one another.

Jigsaws

Jigsaw assignments are those that are broken into "pieces" or sections, but when the sections are put together, they create a whole project. Jigsaws are ideal for team projects because each team member will have the responsibility for completing a defined section. However, they will have to work with the other team members to ensure that the projects are cohesive and filled with continuity. The team will also have to come together if there is a presentation component to the assignment.

Accountability teams

An accountability team can be useful for learners to help each other complete individual assignments. For example, in a research class or a class with a research project requirement, every learner will have their own individual research projects that they will carry out. However, the class can be split into accountability teams where they will provide peer-feedback and support to each other during each step of their research. To ensure that the teams take the accountability piece of the assignment seriously, the role of the accountability team should be laid out by the instructor and made part of the overall grade.

Case studies

Case studies are a team project option. If your online course includes robust and complex case studies that need to be analyzed, for example in a law course or a counseling psychology course that rely on the use of case studies to help learners master the content. Teams can go through the cases and related facts, make arguments for and against, and ask questions. Case studies are often complex and require the breaking down of information to develop potential solutions. Having a team work on them can make the experience more invigorating for the learners, as well as helping to challenge each other's thought processes.

Robust creative works

Often there are assignments that instructors would like learners to work on, but there may not be enough time in the course to complete them with fidelity. This is particularly true in certain online courses of accelerated length. These types of assignments would work well in a team capacity, where each learner could take on a section of the assignment including building a website for information technology, building a prototype for engineering majors, and developing a comprehensive start-up business plan for business majors. Also, with assignments that rely on innovation and creativity, it is often more effective to combine the thoughts and ideas of multiple parties.

Summary

As educators, we often hear about the common misconceptions about the online course experience: working on team assignments, projects, and lacking a strong social presence with the instructor. However, in order to create an effective collaborative and socially influenced online learning environment, the instructor must be provided with a *designer's toolkit* to ensure that their learners are equipped with the tools needed to be successful when participating in team-based tasks. It is also important that the instructor is mindful in how to organize teams effectively and facilitate participatory and peer learning activities. In the next chapter, we will highlight some essential techniques to assess active and experiential learning opportunities.

6
Assessment of Active and Experiential Learning

Overview of Assessing Active and Experiential Learning in Online Courses

The traditional discussion board is typically used in an online course to assess knowledge transfer from instructor to learner or learner-to-learner interaction. Draper et al. (2005) described this relationship between content-area instruction and literacy instruction as a "dualism", and their contention was that teachers must teach learners about how the texts in their disciplines are created and used. In the online setting, the discussion board is a unilateral teaching approach where the instructor's presence and role must stimulate learners to be engaged in meaningful conversation on concepts. Most of the discussion questions must be framed in a way that encourages an effective dialogue around the specific topic or content. At most, discussion board questions tend to be open-ended. Making learner or instructor presence known in the discussion boards must be structured in a way that learners are not overwhelmed by the frequency of the posting or lack of engagement from classmates. Posting either too frequently or less frequently tends to lead to shorter discussions or lack of instructor presence/disconnect to push the conversation forward (Mazzolini & Maddison, 2003). Draper's (2002) work with her content-area colleagues yielded the understanding that some of the strategies suggested by educators were contradictory to the needs of some disciplines.

Since online discussion boards are traditionally text-based, they lack a sense of community and interaction because there is no facial expression or body language to convey engagement with one another – only the content and the perception of what a learner is willing to share. This often leads to misunderstandings between learners and the instructor. Therefore, a rubric would be the most effective tool to assess the interaction and knowledge transfer that goes on in the online discussion board. For example, the rubric tool allows the instructor to provide specific guidelines and expectations regarding learners' participation on the discussion board. The current challenges for educators are to identify which strategies do and do not have merit and to develop their own knowledge of the roles discussion boards play in the disciplinary subject areas in online classrooms.

Some basic techniques on how online discussion boards are assessed are outlined in Table 6.1.

Table 6.1 Techniques to assess online discussion boards

Assessment criteria	Brief description
Participation (Frequency of post and establishing the ground rules)	Individual postings also known as the initial post should have clear and standard guidelines for the online discussion board. For example, "Learners must post their initial post by **Thursday** night by 11p.m ET and also post a follow-up as well as response to at least two other classmate's post by **Sunday** night by 11p.m. ET." It would be also helpful for instructors to include guidelines about format and length of a discussion board. For example, this can be mentioned in a general sense in the prompt as "your responses should be no more than two paragraphs" or as concise as "your responses should be at least 250 words in length and in narrative form". Note: Instructors should also be encouraged to create group discussion boards to facilitate course discussions. Group discussion contains a subset of learners to interact and contribute their thoughts in a smaller cohort.

Point Allocation (How much is this assignment worth?)	Instructors should provide very specific guidelines for evaluating learners and associating a grade for discussion contributions and participation. It would be helpful for the instructor to provide information on the following: • Points based on number of postings • Posts should be submitted in a timely fashion • Length of posts • Well informed response posts to other classmates (not just the typical, "I agree", "Nice post")
Connection Concepts	Instructors should create discussion questions that help assess learners' comprehension of the course topics. This may require learners to include references or citations from readings, lecture materials, or other external resources that may have influenced their rationale or enriched their application of real-world experience.
Stimulating or Clarifying course questions	Instructor presence and facilitation is very important in the online discussion board. It is the instructor's role to stimulate the dialogue and keep learners engaged throughout the duration or length of the discussion board. For example, it would be helpful for instructors to: • create 2–3 guiding discussion questions to continue discussions among learners • provide learner feedback to ensure that their perspective of learning is aligned with understanding the course content.

In this book, our focus has been to go beyond the traditional discussion board and provide ways to actively engage learners in the online course through other 21st-century learning opportunities. We do agree that the benefits of the discussion board allow learners to communicate around processes, brainstorming, sharing ideas about the content, and even reflecting on their experiences. However, recently, we have come to believe that the attention of online learning is now focused on other learning opportunities that we have already discussed in this book. This can be almost directly attributed to the aforementioned issues with online teachers, but there is a more subtle influence – the dilemma of online assessment throughout online education. As we know online assessments are required and are more directly related to what learners know or what the learner needs to know. The debate about the online assessment tools needed for a course is directly affected by the fact that generic skills and strategies are often inappropriate. Addressing, which assessment tools are best for specific initiatives, learning outcomes, and for specific online disciplines has taken center stage in the wider field of online learning today. Researchers have recently encouraged those involved with online instruction to adopt a more complex view of assessment that addresses the demands specific to content areas (Johnson et al., 2011). This follows because deep knowledge of a discipline is best acquired by engaging in the things used by experts in that discipline (Shanahan & Shanahan, 2012). Through online assessment coupled with active learning opportunities provided by the ways inherent in their discipline, learners deepen their knowledge and understanding of the topics within the discipline that pertains to their online coursework.

Formative and Summative Assessments

How do we know our online learners are learning? It is important to have different types of assessments in any online course, including those that are more summative in nature and those that are more formative. Formative assessments are used during the course to ensure that learners are meeting weekly learning objectives. In a traditional course, instructors sometimes use informal observation during class time to observe learners, or have learners complete small homework assignments. In an online class, learning can be observed by their responses on the discussion board, journals and online blog posts. Also, smaller assignments and papers can be required throughout the course which would give learners more opportunities to demonstrate where they are in the learning process.

Summative assessments are more formal and typically are given towards the end of the course as a final assignment. In a traditional bricks and mortar course, summative assessments are the final projects and presentations, or end of unit exams. These are the assignments that tell you if the learner has met the learning objectives of the course. In an online course, instructors can design summative assessments that align well with the available learning technologies within the learning management system (LMS). For example, using the portfolio feature, online learners can create an electronic portfolio that documents their learning throughout the course while highlighting various learning artifacts and key assignments. In an online dance class, learners could record a final performance demonstrating their technique and form of a specific dance genre. The key to creating summative assessments is that they are due at the end of the course with the primary purpose of evaluating whether learners have met the course learning objectives.

It is important to have both formative and summative assignments in online courses so that the instructor is always well aware of how their learners are managing and receiving the course content. Formative assessments are also a practical way to get feedback as an instructor on how effective your teaching has been. Since formative assessments are given during the course, it provides instructors with opportunities to modify learning activities and provide additional support to learners who may require it, without them reaching out directly for support. Summative assessment data can be used by online instructors to determine if any content should be changed during the next course.

Accountability Standards
Developing and communicating learning outcomes

Even though activities related to experiential and active learning are seen as informal learning opportunities by some, it is important to develop and connect each experience to specific course learning outcomes. Bloom's (1956) taxonomy can be used to develop learning objectives based on the level of mastery. As you can see from Figure 6.1, Bloom's Taxonomy was designed

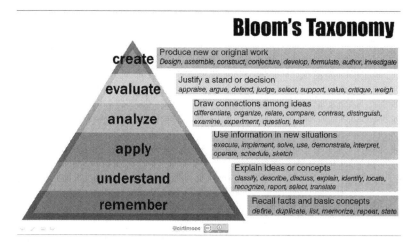

Bloom's Taxonomy

create — Produce new or original work
Design, assemble, construct, conjecture, develop, formulate, author, investigate

evaluate — Justify a stand or decision
appraise, argue, defend, judge, select, support, value, critique, weigh

analyze — Draw connections among ideas
differentiate, organize, relate, compare, contrast, distinguish, examine, experiment, question, test

apply — Use information in new situations
execute, implement, solve, use, demonstrate, interpret, operate, schedule, sketch

understand — Explain ideas or concepts
classify, describe, discuss, explain, identify, locate, recognize, report, select, translate

remember — Recall facts and basic concepts
define, duplicate, list, memorize, repeat, state

Figure 6.1 Bloom's Taxonomy

to move learners from basic understanding to a high level of complexity where new work is being formulated and created by the learner. It is important to create learning objectives that connect to course assignments and learning activity, to ensure that there is an alignment with the assessments.

By having the assessment connected to learning outcomes, the purpose of the assignment will make more sense to learners. This is particularly true for learners in an online course and those based on experiential and active learning activities. Some examples are included in Table 6.2.

Role of instructor

The role of an online instructor can take many different formats. One important role is facilitator of the learning process. In this role, the instructor should question and encourage learners to think more critically about the course content, while making connections with the different experiential and active learning experiences they are engaged in.

It is important to establish expectations for learners so they are aware of how they will be assessed. This includes both summative

Table 6.2 Sample learning outcomes for experiential/active learning

Experiential learning activity	Learning outcome	Assessment
Internship	Learners will be able to interpret basic tax documents	Case study analysis where learners are given a tax situation of a fictional person and must interpret the tax document
Service-learning	Learners will be able to identify housing options of low income families	A knowledge check where learners must answer questions correctly related to the affordable housing programs they learned about at their service site
Learner teaching	Learners will be able to design unit plans	Give learners a grade level and subject-area, and have them create a unit plan

and formative assessments. This is particularly important for online instructors who have to describe assignment guidelines and expectations asynchronously.

Video explanation of assignment guidelines

Sometimes it is difficult for learners to understand what the instructor is attempting to communicate through written text. In a traditional bricks and mortar class, learners are able to ask clarification questions of the instructor while the instructor explains the assignment. In an online course, this cannot be done in the same way; however, through the use of video explanations of assignment guidelines, instructors have the ability to thoroughly explain assignment guidelines, with the use of video, images and text. Learners will also have the ability to watch and listen to the recording multiple times, as they work on the assignment.

Promoting academic integrity

In online courses, special attention must be paid to ensuring that learners are adhering to academic integrity standards within the course. It is very difficult to monitor learners when completing summative and formative assessments. There are some tools that can assist online instructors with protecting the fidelity of learner completion of online work.

Tools to assist

Turnitin is a very useful tool for online instructors who have learners who complete written work. This can include formal papers related to their experiential learning experiences, research papers created for their project and scenario-based learning assignments, or team papers. Turnitin can be embedded into many LMSs, and learners can submit their papers directly into Turnitin. One of the most useful features of engaging learners in the writing process is with the comments that can be left directly on the learner's paper. Additionally, Turnitin shows you how original the learner's work is, and tells the instructor where similar work has been published. The image in Figure 6.2 shows an example of a paper submitted to Turnitin and the originality match.

Online video proctoring monitoring of exams

Depending on the type of exam learners are taking, you may want to ensure that they do not use any outside materials to assist them. The use of an online video proctor monitoring service for exams can assist with this.

Use of textbooks for quizzes

If you do not have the capability of using online proctoring services, you may want to create a time limit for the test, which could limit use of textbooks. Even if the exam is closed-book, learners may be tempted to peep at their notes, and with no one watching, those chances of them doing so are increased.

Figure 6.2 Turnitin is an online assessment tool for written assignments

Examples of Different Assessment Methods with the Different Active and Experiential Learning Strategies

Knowledge checks

Knowledge checks are similar to quizzes; however, the main purpose is to glean how learners are doing in the course. By calling these types of assessments "knowledge checks", as opposed to "quizzes", it removes the pressure that comes with formal tests. Most LMS have integrated systems where you can create a quiz, and if it is multiple choice, it grades automatically directly to the grade center. The online instructor can manipulate settings for these online knowledge checks and decide if it will be timed and if so, for how long, as well as deciding whether learners will be given the option to retake the knowledge check.

The following are examples of appropriate knowledge checks for short writing checks and application assignments:

- Short writing: journals, blogs, discussion boards, reflections;
- Application assignments: projects, authentic (real-world) assessments, case studies.

Virtual presentations

Presenting one's learning in a presentation format is an essential part of many courses. Some instructors may focus on a learner's presentation style while others focus on content. The online forum has the capacity to serve learners well in creating dynamic presentations, as well as presenting material. Presentations allow for learners to be creative in sharing what they have learned at their experiential learning sites or some of the project-based and scenario-based learning activities they participated in. If you are designing virtual presentations for learners, following these steps can be helpful:

Provide guidelines. This includes giving learners specifics on the length of presentation, professional appearance, and how to engage an audience during a presentation. The technology options are endless so it is essential to provide learners with some boundaries and expectations. We have found that shorter presentations of 7–10 minutes result in a higher quality. Two platforms that have worked really well for learners to record and present their materials have been: Present.me (https://present.me/content/) and Knovio (http://www.knovio.com/). Learners may also create presentations in a podcast format using a multimedia app such as Audiolio (https://itunes.apple.com/us/app/audiolio-audio-recorder-text/id403056408?mt=8).

Create virtual space for sharing presentations and getting feedback. One of the benefits of virtual learner presentations is the opportunity for learners to learn from each other. Use a space within your Learning Management System (LMS) for learners to post their presentations and get feedback. It is possible to set up a discussion board forum in an LMS like Blackboard Learn where learners can publicly post the link to the presentation and leave written feedback for their peers. In addition to learners reviewing each other's presentations, the course instructor should view and provide feedback. This feedback can be recorded and uploaded as an MP3 file or written as text.

Key Online Assessment Elements for Active and Experiential Learning Opportunities

The teaching and learning experience can be especially affected by the use of assessments in an online environment. Understanding the role of assessments in active and experiential learning therefore, means understanding under what circumstances what elements can drive learning behavior and what affects learners' learning experiences, their sense of identity and their professional positioning. Instructors can create active and experiential learning strategies based on learner needs and interests by measuring their understanding of the material through online assessment tools. Activities such as diagnostic quizzes, discussions, or polls, when carefully designed and focused on learning objectives, can allow instructors to reveal learners' prior knowledge and monitor comprehension while facilitating learning (Bloom, Hastings & Madaus, 1971).

Online learning provides learners with the opportunity to adapt their education to their lifestyle. Many educators believe that online learning through active and experiential learning opportunities allows learners to collaborate and reach a broader and larger audience. Greater diversity of online assessment will allow the online classroom to extend its reach globally as well as into the local communities. Learners from around the world can connect with one another, which in turn, enriches the learning experience by providing meaningful discussions and multiple perspectives on topics. Incorporating the appropriate assessment tool into learning models/platforms has helped instructors to maximize the available resources and consider new approaches to instructional design (Lei & Gupta, 2010). Active learning and experiential learning techniques have emerged as strategies for instructors to promote engagement among multiple disciplines and have been able to cater to a variety of learning styles.

The Role of Assessments in Active Learning

Assessments play a major role in the active learning process. They provide a basis for learners and instructors to reflect and convey that learning has taken place and can immediately show areas of improvements. Aligning the assessment with active learning assignments allows for a "reflective process that ensures continued growth long after specific learning opportunities have been completed" (Bassett & Jackson, 1994, p. 73). For instance, Hu and Wolniak (2010) used items measuring academic engagement that assessed working and discussing with other learners, discussing work with instructors, and working harder than expected to meet expectations. On the other hand, social engagement was measured by assessing learner involvement in extracurricular and enrichment activities (Hu & Wolniak, 2010). Therefore, the use of active-learning techniques to assess learners can be organized in the following ways for the online classroom:

- **Observations:** A type of assessment based on a performance task that can be observed by the instructor or as a peer-review by other learners in the class. This type of assessment tool informs the learner about their learning growth and/or progression as well as easily identifying learning challenges.
- **Checklists or self-assessments:** A type of assessment that instructors can use to allow learners to complete self-reflective assignments (e.g. essays, article reviews, blogs, discussions, etc.). Requiring learners to complete a checklist in the form of a questionnaire or allow them to have the opportunity to reflect on course materials informs the teacher about individual achievement and to identify any learning gaps.

- **Sample work/portfolios:** A type of assessment where learners either compile a collection of their best work that reflects on course understanding or acquired skills, or can be used as a final evaluation of learner work for a particular program progression. This type of assessment tool informs the instructor about consistent course themes, patterns, that align with learning objectives for learner mastery.
- **Tests/quizzes:** A type of assessment that informs the instructor immediately about the effectiveness of their teaching strategies or how the course material is structured. For example, in the online environment instructors can create knowledge checks to assess any learner at any point in their learning around the course content. Online tests and quizzes are traditionally used and allow for immediate feedback from the instructor by providing a quick snapshot of the learner's comprehensive learning profile (e.g. abilities, needs, interests or preferences).

The Role of Assessments in Experiential Learning

While learner engagement has a well-established role in learning, comprehension, and academic performance (Kuh, 2008), experiential learning has also been shown to be closely related to career or occupational outcomes. There are several ways to assess experiential learning activities in the online classroom. Similar to active learning, most of these assessment methods are based on individual/group reflections and reflective writing assignments that allow learners to focus their learning on particular events or scenarios while also presenting a final deliverable at the end of the course. More specifically, oral presentations prove to be a great assessment to inform instructors of the key learning points that were either achieved or were a challenge among learners. Again, since learners are working on various assignments at different times, the instructor cannot assume that every learning experience will be valued in the same way. According to Wurdinger, with the "appropriate assessment tool, such as a self-assessment, the educator might not ever realize that significant learning occurred. Therefore, educators should search for assessment techniques that measure more than just the ability to remember information" (2005, p. 69). The use of experiential techniques to assess learning can be organized in the following ways:

- **Oral presentation/oral exam:** A type of assessment that informs the instructor about the comprehensive learning experiences. This assessment tool is usually administered at the end of the course as a reflective presentation of the learning journey and assesses how learners were able to clearly articulate their learning/findings.
- **On-the job internship:** A type of assessment that informs the instructor about the work-related environment and any skills acquired at the internship. For example, learners can participate in on-the-job learning experience where they apply the course content learned to their work environment. Learners may be asked to track their leaning using an online blogging tool, and writing centered around specific questions outlined by the instructor.
- **Role playing exercises:** A type of assessment that allows the learner to assume a role of another individual and provide a particular content scenario, issue, or simulation. The instructor would be able to assess the learner's ability to transfer knowledge learned and be able to compile and synthesize a perspective based on the course content.
- **Interviewing experts in the field:** A type of assessment tool most commonly used in the social sciences and educational online course disciplines where learners have the opportunity to locate and interview an expert in their field. One caveat to this assessment tool is that the instructor is able to assess how learners are able to connect and apply course content to novel and new issues around a particular assignment given. Technology tools tend to play a major role in ensuring the interview is captured or transcribed as a way to make learning connections.

- **Workplace recommendations for improvement:** A type of assessment that informs the instructor that the learner is able to identify and investigate a problem that the learner may be experiencing in their workplace or potential workplace. This assessment tool allows the learner to be able to map out the process or steps to recommend areas of improvement. In other words, the learners have to take on the perspective that they are change agents who want to apply their expertise of the situation by connecting ideas and knowledge based on the course content that is being presented.

Sample Adaptive Learning Tools for Online Assessments

According to Gardner (1983), intelligence can be measured based on the skills that they are able to use to gain new knowledge and solve problems. Gardner believes that there are eight different types of learning styles:

1. **Verbal-Linguistic**/Word Smart: Learners in this learning category tend to have a learning style that grasps the content by engaging in readings, discussions, written assignment, and oral/verbal presentations.
2. **Logical-Mathematical**/Logic Smart: Learners in this learning category tend to learn best by engaging in activities that allow them to connect relationships, identify patterns or themes, etc.
3. **Visual-Spatial**/Picture Smart: Learners in this learning category tend to learn best through visual demonstrations as well as from diagrams, images and other visual aids.
4. **Auditory-Musical**/Music Smart: Learners in this learning category tend to learn best by incorporating audio aids, such as music in the form of hearing or singing of the course content.
5. **Bodily-Kinesthetic**/Body Smart: Learners in this learning category tend to learn best through touch or by moving around. Hands-on lab demonstrations, gaming, or site visits allow these learners to gather and process information of the course content.

6. **Interpersonal**/People Smart: Learners in this learning category tend to learn best from others by working in teams or groups that allow them to collaborate, discuss, and share knowledge that they learn.

7. **Intrapersonal**/Self Smart: Learners in this learning category tend to learn best by having self-directed goals or activities that allow them to organize and process their knowledge internally.

8. **Naturalistic**/Nature Smart: Learners in this learning category tend to learn best by working in the external environment (outside the classroom experiences). In some online courses, instructors can encourage learners to participate in city walks or field experiences that get them "outside" and interacting with the knowledge learning in the course.

Learning Tools for Assessments

Table 6.3 provides different examples of how online instructors can assess the experiential and active learning of their learners outside of their LMS. Additionally, many of these types of assessment will also add to the learner engagement element of the course and allow learners the opportunity to demonstrate their learning, in different ways. Please note that many of these tools contain their own data that can serve as learning analytics to identify and track areas of learner strengthens and areas needing improvement.

Table 6.3 Examples of how online instructors can assess the experiential and active learning of their learners outside of their LMS

Tool	Website	Why Use this Tool
VoiceThread	http://voicethread.com/	Instructors can embed quiz questions within lecture content. Learners have the opportunity to ask questions and received immediate feedback from the instructor.
Qualtrics	http://www.qualtrics.com/	Learning analytics tool that allows both instructor and learners to view and track learning progress and online activity.

Poll Everywhere	https://www. pollevery where.com/	A survey creation tool that instructors can use to create online assessments to embed into their online course. This platform also has a learning analytics capability to track learner responses.
Survey Monkey	https://www. surveymonkey. com/	Another survey creation tool to create online assessments. Instructors can also generate web-based reports for an individual learner or for the entire course.
Google Forms	https://www. google.com/ forms/about/	Free open source tools where instructions can create and embed surveys, questionnaires, and even knowledge checks for learners to assess understanding of key course concepts.
Respondus	https://www. respondus. com/	An assessment tool for creating and managing online exams that can be uploaded directly to most learning management systems.
Interactive Rubrics (Anneberg Foundation)	http://www. learner.org/ workshops/ hswriting/ interactives/ rubric/	A rubric tool that allows the instructor to create a customized rubric for their course's learning activities and assignments.
Slack	https://slack. com/?story= video&v=1	Instantmessaging mobile app for instructors to be able to provide immediate feedback or answer any course questions to learners in real-time rather than sending an email or posting to a discussion board. This tool also allows for file sharing so that instructors can use this tool to collaborate with learners and increase instructor presence and interaction.

Summary

In this final chapter, we outlined important techniques and resources that can be used to monitor as well as evaluate student performance that involve active and experiential learning opportunities. These diverse assessment methods will continue to evolve over time, especially in online learning environments where timely and constructive feedback is key. Nevertheless, it is important for online instructors to be able to align every assessment and assignment to the course learning outcomes. This unpretentious task can be done simply by asking: What type of assessment data am I seeking from the assignment (formative versus summative)? Why should the assignment be assessed? When should the assignment be assessed? How should the assignment be assessed?, and finally, Who is the assignment assessing (e.g. individual, peer-to-peer, experience, etc.)? The answers to these questions will reveal how instructors should create effective assessments that measure student learning: prior, during, and after the online learning experience.

As this book comes to a conclusion, we hope that you have found a plethora of practical, valuable, and useful ideas to include or expand active and experiential learning activities in your online and hybrid courses. We are confident that through the use of some or all of the strategies we explored in this book including project and scenario-based learning, service-learning, gaming, social media, peer and participatory learning, and 21st century assessment practices, your learners will be engaged, inspired, and comprehensively connected with the course content that will drive overall student success and a meaningful educational experience.

References

Abedi, M. & Badragheh, A. (2011). Distance learning: Definitions and applications. *Journal of American Science*, 7(4), 302–306.

Aebersold, M. & Tschannen, D. (2013). Simulation in nursing practice: the impact on patient care. *The Online Journal of Issues in Nursing*, 18(2) manuscript 6. doi: 10.3912/OJIN.

Allen, I.E. & Seaman, J. (2013). *Changing Course: Ten years of tracking online education in the United States.* Babson Park, MA: Babson Survey Research Group and Quahog Research Group.

Alliance for Excellence in Education (All4Ed). (2010). *High School Dropouts in America.* Retrieved from: http://all4ed.org/wp-content/uploads/HighSchoolDropouts.pdf

Appana, S. (2008). A Review of benefits and limitations of online learning in the context of the student, the instructor, and the tenured faculty. *International JI on E-Learning*, 7(1), 22.

Association of Experiential Education. (2015). *What is Experiential Education? (What is EE).* Retrieved from http://www.aee.org/what-is-ee

Barron, B. & Darling-Hammond, L. (2008). Teaching for meaningful learning: A review of research on inquiry-based and cooperative learning (PDF).

Bartle, R. (2004). *Designing Virtual Worlds.* Boston: New Riders Publishing.

Bassett, D.S. & Jackson, L. (1994). Applying the model to a variety of adult learning situations. In L. Jackson. & R.S. Caffarella (Eds.). *Experiential Learning: A new approach* (pp. 73–86). San Francisco: Jossey-Bass.

Bigatel, P. & Williams, V. (2015). Measuring student engagement in an online program. *Online Journal of Distance Learning Administration*, 18 (2).

Bloom, B.S. (Ed.). Engelhart, M.D., Furst, E.J., Hill, W.H. & Krathwohl, D.R. (1956). *Taxonomy of Educational Objectives, Handbook I: The Cognitive Domain.* New York: David McKay Co Inc.

Bloom, B.S., Hastings, J.T. & Madaus, G.F. (1971). *Handbook of Formative and Summative Evaluation of Student Learning.* New York: McGraw-Hill.

Bloom, S. (Ed.). (1956). *Taxonomy of Educational Objectives, the classification of educational goals – Handbook I: Cognitive Domain.* New York: McKay.

Bonwell, C.C. & Eison, J.A. (1991). *Active learning: Creating excitement in the classroom. ASHE-ERIC Higher Education Report No. 1.* Washington, DC: The George Washington University.

Bridgeland, J.M., Dilulio, J.J. & Morison, K.B. (2006). *The Silent Epidemic: Perspectives of high school dropouts.* Retrieved from https://docs.gatesfoundation.org/Documents/TheSilentEpidemic3-06Final.pdf

Brinthaupt, T.M., Fisher, L.S., Gardner, J.G., Raffo, D.M. & Woodard, J.B. (2011). What the best online teachers should do. *Journal of Online Learning and Teaching*, 7, 515–524.

Brown, J.S., Collins, A. & Duguid, P. (1989). Situated cognition and the culture of learning. *Educational Researcher*, 18(1), 32–42.

Buck Institute for Education (BIE). (2015). *Why Project Based Learning (PBL)?* Retrieved from http://www.bie.org/about/what_pbl

Buckingham, D. (Ed). (2006). *Youth Identity and Digital Media.* Cambridge, MA: MIT Press.

Chee, Y.S. (2007). Embodiment, embeddedness, and experience: Game-based learning and the construction of identity. *Research and Practice in Technology Enhanced Learning*, 2(1), 3–30.

Cooperative Education and Internship Association. (2015). *History of Cooperative Education and Internships.* Retrieved September 13, 2016, from http://www.ceiainc.org/about/history/

Czerkawski, B. (2014). Designing deeper learning experiences for online instruction. *Journal of Interactive Online Learning*, 13(2).

Dede, C. (2007). *Transforming Education for the 21st Century: New pedagogies that help all students attain sophisticated learning outcomes.* Commissioned by the NCSU Friday Institute, February.

Dewey, J. (1915). *The School and Society.* Chicago, IL: The University of Chicago Press.

Dewey, J. (1933). *How We Think.* Boston, MA: Heath.

Dewey, J. (1938). *Experience and Education.* New York, NY: The Macmillan Company.

Dingel, M. & Wei, W. (2014). Influences on peer evaluation in a group project: An exploration of leadership, demographics and course performance. *Assessment & Evaluation in Higher Education*, 39(6), 729–742.

Draper, R.J. (2002). Every teacher a literacy teacher? An analysis of the literacy-related messages in secondary methods textbooks. *Journal of Literacy Research*, 34, 357–384.

Draper, R.J., Smith, L.K., Hall, K.M. & Siebert, D. (2005). What's more important – literacy or content? Confronting the literacy–content dualism. *Action in Teacher Education*, 27(2), 12–21.

Evans, D. & Taylor, J. (2005). The role of user scenarios as the central piece of the development jigsaw puzzle. In J. Attewell & C. Savill-Smith (Eds.). *Mobile Learning Anytime Everywhere.* London: Learning and Skills Development Agency.

Figueira, A. & Leal, H. (2013). An online tool to manage and assess collaborative group work. *Proceedings of The International Conference on E-Learning*, 112–120.

Foster, A. & Mishra, P. (2011). Games, claims, genres and learning. In Information Resources Management Association USA (Ed.). *Gaming and Simulations: Concepts, methodologies, tools, and application*, 1, 497–513: IGI Global.

Gardner, H. (1983). *Frames of Mind.* New York: Basic Books.

Garrison, D.R., Anderson, T. & Archer, W. (2001). Critical thinking, cognitive presence, and computer conferencing in distance education. *American Journal of Distance Education*, 15(1), 7–23.

Gee, J.P. (2003). *What Video Games Have to Teach Us about Learning and Literacy.* New York: Palgrave Macmillan.

Gee, J.P. (2004). *Situated Language and Learning: A critique of traditional schooling.* New York: Routledge.

Glatthorn, Allan A. (1993) Outcome based education: Reform and the curriculum process. *Journal of Curriculum and Supervision*, 8(4), 354–363.

Gros, B. (2007). Digital games in education: The design of games-based learning. *Environments – Journal of Research on Technology in Education*, 1–21.

Guthrie, K.L. & McCracken, H. (2010). Teaching and learning social justice through online service-learning courses. *The International Review of Research in Open and Distance Learning*, 11(3), 78–94.

Heeter, C. (2009). Play styles and learning. In R. Ferdig (Ed.). *Handbook of Research on Electronic Gaming in Education* (pp. 826–846). Hershey, PA: Information Science Reference.

Heeter, C., Magerko, B., Medler, B. & Fitzgerald, J. (2009). Game design and the challenge-avoiding "Validator" player type. *International Journal of Gaming and Computer Mediated Simulations*, 1(3), 53–67.

Hew, K. & Brush, T. (2007). Integrating technology into k-12 teaching and learning: Current knowledge gaps and recommendations for future research. *Education Technology Research Development*, 55, 223–252.

Hirumi, A. (2002). The design and sequencing of E-learning interactions: A grounded approach. *International Journal on E-learning*, 1(1), 19–27.

Hu, S. & Wolniak, G.C. (2010). Initial evidence on the influence of college student engagement on early career earnings. *Research in Higher Education*, 51(8), 750–766.

Hu, S. & Wolniak, G.C. (2013). College student engagement and early career earnings: Differences by gender, race/ethnicity, and academic preparation. *The Review of Higher Education*, 36(2), 211–233.

Huang, T. & Plass, J. (2009). *Microsoft Research: History of play in education*. New York: Games for Learning Institute.

Jacobson, J., Oravecz, L., Falk, A. & Osteen, P. (2011). Proximate outcomes of service-learning among family studies undergraduates. *Family Science Review*, 16(1), 22–33.

Jacoby, B. (1999). Partnerships for service learning. *New Directions for Student Services*, 87, 18–35.

Jenkins, H., Purushotma, R., Clinton, K. & Robison, A. (2009). *Confronting the Challenges of Participatory Culture: Media education for the 21st century*. Cambridge, MA: MIT Press.

Johnson, H.H., Watson, P.P., Delahunty, T.T., McSwiggen, P.P. & Smith, T.T. (2011). What it is they do: Differentiating knowledge and literacy practices across content disciplines. *Journal of Adolescent & Adult Literacy*, 55(2), 100–109. doi:10.1002/JAAL.00013.

Klopfer, E. (2008) *Augmented Learning: Research and design of mobile educational games*. Cambridge, MA: MIT Press.

Kolb, D.A. 1984. *Experiential Learning: Experience as the source of learning and development*. Englewood Cliffs, NJ: Prentice-Hall.

Kuh, G.D. (2008). *High-Impact Educational Practices: What they are, who has access to them, and why they matter*. Washington, DC: Association of American Colleges and Universities.

Leblanc, G. (2004). Enhancing intrinsic motivation through the use of a token economy. *Essays in Education*, 11(1).

Lei, S.A. & Gupta, R.K. (2010). College distance education courses. *Distance Education*, 130, 616–631.

Mazzolini, M. & Maddison, S. (2003). Sage, guide or ghost? The effect of instructor intervention on student participation in online discussion forums. *Computers & Education*, 40, 237.

Nakamura, J. & Csikszentimihalyi, M. (2002). Concept of flow. In C.R. Snyder & S. Lopez (Eds.). *Handbook of Positive Psychology* (pp. 89–105). New York, NY: Oxford University Press.

National Association of Colleges and Employers. (2011). Position Statement: US Internships. Retrieved September 10, 2016, from http://www.naceweb.org/advocacy/position-statements/united-states-internships.aspx.

Pacansky-Brock, M. (2013). *Best Practices for Teaching with Emerging Technologies.* New York: Routledge.

Panofsky, C.P. (2003). *Vygotsky's Educational Theory in Cultural Context: The relations of learning and student social class: toward re-socializing sociocultural learning theory.* New York, NY: Cambridge University Press.

Quaye, S. & Harper, S. (2015). *Student Engagement in Higher Education.* New York, NY: Routledge.

Rourke, L., Anderson, T., Garrison, D.R. & Archer, W. (2001). Assessing social presence in asynchronous text-based computer conferencing. *The Journal of Distance Education*, 14, 50–71.

Ryan, R.M. & Deci, E.L. (2000). Self-determination theory and the facilitation of intrinsic motivation, social development, and well-being. *American Psychologist*, 55, 68–78.

Salen, K. & Zimmerman, E. (2003). *Rules of Play: Game design fundamentals.* Cambridge, MA: MIT Press.

Shanahan, T. & Shanahan, C. (2012). What is disciplinary literacy and why does it matter? *Topics in Language Disorders*, 32(1), 7–18.

Smith, G.G., Sorensen, C., Gump, A., Heindel, A.J., Caris, M. & Martinez, C.D. (2011). Overcoming student resistance to group work: Online versus face-to-face. *Internet & Higher Education*, 14(2), 121–128.

Sorin, R., Errington, E., Ireland, L., Nickson, A. & Caltabiano, M. (2012). Embedding graduate attributes through scenario-based learning. *Journal of the NUS Teaching Academy*, 2(4), 192–205.

Squire, K. (2006). From content to context: Videogames as designed experience. *Educational Researcher*, 35(8), 19–29.

Vygotsky, L.S. (1979). Consciousness as a problem in the psychology of behavior. *Soviet Psychology*, 17, 3–35.

Wagner, T. (2012). *Creating Innovators: The making of young people who will change the world.* New York: Scribner.

Waldner, L.S., Widener, M.C. & McGorry, S.Y. (2012). E-Service-Learning: The evolution of service-learning to engage a growing online student population. *Journal of Higher Education Outreach and Engagement*, 16(2), 123–150.

Ward, M.E., Peters, G. & Shelley, K. (2010). Student and faculty perceptions of the quality of online learning experiences. *International Review of Research in Open and Distance Learning*, 11(3), 57–77.

Wurdinger, D.D. & Carlson, J.A. (2010). *Teaching for Experiential Learning: Five approaches that work.* Lanham, MD: Rowman & Littlefield Education.

Wurdinger, S.D. (2005). *Using Experiential Learning in the Classroom.* Lanham, MD: Scarecrow Education.

Yee, N. (2004). *Motivations of Play in MMORPGs.* Retrieved from http://www.nickyee.com/daedalus/motivations.pdf

Index

abstract conceptualization 13–14
academic integrity, promoting 80
accountability standards 77–81
accountability teams 70
Achievers 51, 52
active citizenry 19
active experimentation 2, 13–14
active learning
    definition 2, 3
    passive learning vs. 3–4
affinity spaces 10, 39
Agreeadate 30–1
Allen, I.E. 8
alternate identities 4, 50
American Association of Colleges of
    Pharmacy (AACP) 32
American Bar Association 32
American Health Information
    Management Association 32
American Nurses Association 32
Anderson, T. 62
Anneberg Foundation 89
application assignments 81–2
apprenticeship 38
Archer, W. 62
Articulate Storyline 41
assessment 73–89
    accountability standards 77–81
    of discussion boards 74–5
    examples of methods 81–3
    formative 76–7, 79
    key elements 83–4
    learning tools for 87–9
    overview 73–6
    role in active learning 84–5
    role in experiential learning 85–7
    summative 76–7, 78–9
    tools 80
assignment guidelines, video
    explanation of 79
Association for Experiential
    Education 14, 32
Association of International Education
    Administrators 32

Association for Teacher Educators 32
asynchronous learning, synchronous
    learning vs. 8–9
attrition 6
Audiolio 82
avatars 50, 54

Barron, B. 36
Bartle, Richard 51
Blackboard 68
Blackboard Learn 83
blogs 20–7
    tools 26–7
Bloom, S. 77
Bloom's Taxonomy of Higher Order
    Thinking 7, 77–8
Buck Institute for Education 36
Buckingham, D. 37
business, experiential learning activities
    in 21

Campus Compact 32
Careless 51
case studies 70–1
checklists 84
choice learning activities 44
civic contribution 19
coaches, teachers as 36
Code Spell 57
collaboration, digital tools for 66–9
collective competencies 62
communication, in team
    projects 67–8
communication skills 45, 56, 62
communities of practice 10
community, engaging with 13
Community of Inquiry Framework 62
community organizations, meeting
    with 28–9
competition 55
computer adaptive learning 50
concrete experience 2, 13–14
co-operative education (co-ops) 14–15,
    19, 21–3

Cooperative Education and Internship
    Association 15, 32
cooperative learning
    benefits 61
    challenges 61–2
    see also team projects
course content, continuity in delivery 28
creative expression 38
creative works, robust 71
creative writing 40
critical thinking skills 56
Csikszentimihalyi, M. 45
cultural technologies 37–8
current events, using 40
curriculum design 54–5

Dale's cone of learning 3–4
Darling-Hammond, L. 36
data, using 40
debates 40
Deci, E.L. 43–4
decision-making skills 45
Design a Parachute 57
Dewey, John 2, 7, 13, 19
Dewey's theory of experiential
    learning 7
diagnostic quizzes 83
digital games *see* games
discussion boards 63, 65, 67, 73–4, 83
    assessment 74–5
    Doodle 29–30
doodling 69
Draper, R.J. 73
Dreambox Learning 57

e-learning platforms 55
education, experiential learning
    activities in 19
email 68
engagement 56
    measurement 84
Evans, D. 39
experiential education, definition 2
experiential learning 13–33
    definition 2, 14
    importance in online courses 18
    instructor's role in organizing in
        online courses 30–1
    models 2, 13–14
    resources for coordinating
        placements 31–3

role of assessments in 85–7
technology tools in facilitating in
    online courses 20–31
types 14–23
exploratory walks 40
Explorers 51–3
EyeJot 68

Facebook 38
facilitator, instructor/teacher as 36, 37,
    39, 78–9
feedback
    peer 64, 70
    on presentations 82–3
    providing learners with 28
    in scenario-based learning 42, 43
    on teaching 77
field experiences 2
file exchange 68
file sharing areas 63
flexible learning environments,
    opportunities for 8–9
flow channel 45
flow theory 45
Food Force 51, 57
forming abstract concepts *see* abstract
    conceptualization
Fuze 31

game play 49
    motivation role in 53–4
    styles 50–3
game-based learning 47–9
    applications 5
game-based research 48
games
    definition 50
    design 54–5
    examples 57
    implementing in online learning
        environment 55–6
    tools 56–7
gamification 1–2, 47–57
gaming scenario 41
Gardner, H. 87
Garrison, D.R. 62
Gee, J.P. 10, 59
Google Docs 38, 68
Google Forms 31, 89
Google Hangouts 31, 67
Google Slides 69

Grand Theft Auto 52
group dynamics, facilitating 63
group projects *see* team projects
groups, working in 36
Guthrie, K.L. 19

hands-on experience 18
Harper, S. 1
health professions, experiential learning
    activities in 20
Heeter, C. 51, 55
Hu, S. 84
human services, experiential learning
    activities in 20

iCivics 57
identities
    alternate 4, 50
    changing 56
    multiple 35
innovation 38, 46
inquiry-based learning 2
Instagram 38, 59
Institute for International Education 32
instructional design 4
instructional strategies 9
instructor role
    in designing team project 63–6
    as facilitator 36, 37, 39, 78–9
    in organizing experiential learning in
        online courses 30–1
Interactive Rubrics 89
International Association for Research on
    Service-Learning and Community
    Engagement 32
internships 2, 15–16, 86
    assessment 79
    sharing learning 25
interpersonal learning style 88
interviews, of experts 86
intrapersonal learning style 88
issue-based scenario 41

Jacoby, B. 16
Jenkins, H. 39–40, 59
Jigsaw assignments 64, 70
Journalate 27
journals, online *see* online journals

Klopfer, E. 50
Knovio 69, 82

knowledge
    management 56
    types of 39
knowledge checks 81, 85
Kolb, David 2, 13

LaTeX 59
learner control 36
learner teaching, assessment 79
learning
    from experience 13
    psychology of 49–50
    socio-cultural view 35–6
learning games 53
learning management systems (LMS) 6,
    63, 66, 68
    assessment in 77, 81, 82–3
learning objectives 77–8
learning outcomes 77–8, 79
learning revolution 10
learning space, need for new type of 10–11
learning styles 3–4, 54–5, 87–8
Leblanc, G. 56
Lightt 27
literacy instruction 73
logic smart learners 87
logical-mathematical learning style 87
Lost 51

McCracken, H. 19
materials, creating, sharing and
    storing 68–9
math, using 40
mentorship 38
    informal 35
Minecraft 52, 57
motivation
    extrinsic 44–5, 52, 54–5
    intrinsic 44, 52, 54–5, 56
    role in game play 53–4
    role in learning 43–5, 54–5, 56
music smart learners 87
Myers-Briggs personality inventory 65

Nakamura, J. 45
National Association of Colleges and
    Employers 15, 32
National Association of International
    Educators 32
National Business Education
    Association 33

National Education Association 33
National Society for Experiential
    Education 33
networking 46

observation and reflection *see* reflective
    observation
observations, in assessment 84
online enrollments 8
online journals 20, 25
    tools 26–7
online learners, rationale for engaging 5–8
online video proctor monitoring 80
oral presentations 40, 85–6

Pacansky-Brock, Michelle 5–6
pairs, working in 36
participation, forms and routes of 39
participatory cultures 10–11, 49, 50, 59
passive learning, active learning vs. 3–4
peer feedback system 64
peer learning 54
    assignment examples 70–1
    benefits 61
    challenges 61–2
    see also team projects
peer-to-peer interaction 4
Penzu 27
people smart learners 88
performance support 56
Piazza 59
Pinterest 59
place-based education 2
placements, finding for learners 31–3
Plato 49
play
    definition 49
    psychology of 49–50
player types 50–3
PocketVideo 26–7
podcasts 82
Poll Everywhere 89
polls 83
portfolios 77, 85
PowerPoint files 69
practicums 2, 16
    sharing learning 25
preference inventories 65
presentations
    oral 40, 85–6
    in team projects 69
    virtual 82–3
Present.me 82

problem-based learning 2
problem-based scenario 40
problem-solving skills 55, 56
problems, realistic 36
professionalism, practice at 18–19
project-based learning (PBL) 2, 35–9, 45, 46
    elements 37
    examples 40
projective selves 4, 50

Qualtrics 88
Quaye, S. 1
Quest Atlantis Remixed 57
questionnaires 84
quizzes 85
    creating 81

random selection 66
RandomList 66
real-world connections, making 18
reflective observation 2, 13–14
reflective thinking 13
Respondus 89
retention 6
role play 37, 40, 41, 53, 86
Rourke, L. 62
rubrics 74
Rules, Play and Culture framework 56
Ryan, R.M. 43–4

Salen, K. 56
sample work 85
sandbox games 52
scenario-based learning (SBL) 35–6,
    39–43, 46
    content type 43
    definition 39
    resources 42–3
    types of scenario 40–1
scheduling, tools 31
schools dropout rate 56
science experiments 40
Seaman, J. 8
Second Life 53–4
Self Determination Theory (SDT) 43–4
self-assessments 84
self-directed learning 53
self-reflection 4, 84
Self-Validators 51, 52, 53
service-learning 2, 16–17, 19, 21–3
    assessment 79
    reflecting on service experience 20
short writing checks 81–2

simulations 1
site supervisors, meeting 28–9
site visits 40
skill-based scenario 40
skills, needed in education 55
Slack 89
social interactions 19, 35, 54, 55
social media 38, 47, 58–9
    examples of tools 59
social positioning 56
social presence 19, 62
social technologies 37–8
Sorin, R. 40
speculative scenario 41
study abroad 2, 17, 21–3
summative assessments 56–7
Survey Monkey 89
synchronous learning, asynchronous
    learning vs. 8–9

Taylor, J. 39
team dynamics, facilitating 63
team projects
    assigning grades 64
    assignment examples 70–1
    benefits 61
    challenges 61–2
    creating teams 65–6
    designing in online courses 62–3
    digital tools for collaboration 66–9
    expectations for individual
        contributions 64
    numbers in teams 66
    online instructor's role in designing
        63–6
tests, online 85

textbooks, use for quizzes 80
theory of experiential learning 7
transformative play 49–50
trouble-shooting skills 55
Turnitin 80, 81
Twitter 38, 59

video conferencing 27–9
    scheduling in asynchronous online
        courses 29–31
    tools 31, 67
virtual blogs see blogs
virtual presentations 82–3
virtual team space, creating 63
virtual worlds 38, 50, 53–4
visual-spatial learning style 87
vlogs 20–6
    tools 26–7
Voicethread 24, 27, 69, 88
Vygotsky, Leo 35, 36, 38, 49

WACE 33
web conferencing 27
Wolniak, G.C. 84
word smart learners 87
wordle.net 17
WordPress 27
workplace recommendations 87
Wurdinger, S.D. 85–6

Yee, Nick 51
YouTube 38, 59

Zimmerman, E. 56
zone of proximal development 49
Zoom 31, 67